RYA
Instru

by Amanda van Santen
RYA Chief Instructor, Dinghy & Windsurfing
Additional words by Andy Carly

© RYA 2010
First Published 2010
Reprinted August 2013
The Royal Yachting Association
RYA House, Ensign Way, Hamble,
Southampton SO31 4YA
Tel: 0844 556 9555
Fax: 0844 556 9516
Email: publications@rya.org.uk
Web: www.rya.org.uk
Follow us on Twitter @RYAPublications
ISBN: 978-1906-435-639
RYA Order Code: W33

Totally Chlorine Free   **Sustainable Forests**

A CIP record of this book is available from the British Library

Note: While all reasonable care has been taken in the preparation of this book, the publisher takes no responsibility for the use of the methods or products or contracts described in the book.

Telephone 0844 556 9555 for a free copy of our Publications Catalogue.

Cover Design: Pete Galvin
Illustrations: Creativebyte
Typeset: Creativebyte
Proofreading and indexing: Alan Thatcher
Printed in China through: World Print
Acknowledgements: Mark Warner, Paul Wyeth, UKSA, Simon Bornhoft, Peter Van Santen, Richard Langdon and Laurence West. Thank you to all RYA Trainers and Coaches for their input and time in helping to produce this revised handbook.

Contents

RYA Code of Conduct for Instructors, Trainers and Coaches

Sports training and coaching helps the development of individuals through improving their performance. This is achieved by:

- Identifying and meeting the needs of individuals.
- Improving performance through a progressing programme of safe, guided practice, measured performance and/or competition.
- Creating an environment in which individuals are motivated to maintain participation and improve performance.

Instructors, Trainers and Coaches should comply with the principles of good practice listed below. They must:

- If working with young people under the age of 18, have read and understood the Child Protection Policy as detailed on the RYA website at www.rya.org.uk
- Respect the rights, dignity and worth of every person and treat everyone equally within the context of their sport.
- Place the well-being and safety of the student above the development of performance. They should follow all guidelines laid down by the sport's governing body and hold appropriate insurance cover.
- Develop an appropriate working relationship with students (especially children), based on mutual trust and respect and not exert undue influence to obtain personal benefit or reward.
- Encourage and guide students to accept responsibility for their own behaviour and performance.
- Hold relevant up to date and nationally recognised governing body qualifications.
- Ensure that the activities they direct or advocate are appropriate for the age, maturity, experience and ability of the individual.
- At the outset, clarify with students (and, where appropriate, their parents) exactly what is expected of them and what they are entitled to expect.
- Always promote the positive aspects of the sport (eg. courtesy to other water users).
- Consistently display high standards of behaviour and appearance.

RYA Organisation

RYA Affiliated Clubs and Initiatives

Affiliated Clubs

Affiliated clubs have been at the very heart of the RYA since its foundation in 1875, and a large part of RYA work is still devoted to their promotion and protection. Any club with an RYA specified boating interest may apply to the RYA for affiliation namely:

- Windsurfing.
- Dinghy Sailing (cruising and racing).
- Yacht Sailing (cruising and racing).
- Motor cruising.
- Sportsboats and RIBs.
- Personal watercraft.
- Powerboat racing.
- Inland Waterways.

It is normally a requirement that a club applying for affiliation has at least 30 members. For full affiliation, a club must have democratically elected officers and a constitution showing that no outside body has control over its affairs. Fully affiliated clubs have one vote for each £1 of affiliation fees paid in voting rights on RYA matters. Clubs that cannot demonstrate democratic process or independence may apply for restricted affiliation, a separate category with no voting rights. For further information about becoming affiliated to the RYA or the benefits of doing so, please contact the RYA at info@rya.org.uk

Team15

A nationwide network of clubs where windsurfers aged 15 and under get together every week, improve their windsurfing skills and have a great time. Using the RYA Youth Windsurfing Logbook (W1) as guidance, appropriately qualified instructors and coaches can sign off proficiency levels including Stages 1 to 4, Start Racing and Intermediate Racing certificates as part of club activities. All Team15 clubs operate at recognised RYA windsurfing centres and are run by RYA qualified windsurfing instructors who are encouraged to take their racing instructor qualification, especially if their club is interested in taking part in inter-club challenges.

Team15 has a softly, softly approach to competition and, while there is no pressure to compete, each Team15 club has the opportunity to enter a specially selected team of 15 (how Team15 got its name) who represent their club at four local inter-club challenges annually. Teams of up to 15 children, all aged 15 or under, represent their club with the aim of winning their zone series.

All inter-club challenges are very friendly events and competition is pitched to cater for all levels of ability, including beginners. The winning team in each competition zone after four inter-club challenges is invited to the annual Team15 Champions Cup for a weekend of fun racing to determine the National Champion Team.

OnBoard

Sailing and windsurfing are fun and give young people an early opportunity to develop confidence, independence and a sense of purpose. But it's not always easy to get started. OnBoard is a nationwide programme that is making it easier for young people to go sailing and windsurfing and get involved in a variety of local activities. It is co-ordinated by the RYA, supported by industry and the sports, and delivered locally by RYA Training Centres. Over a ten year period the programme aims to introduce a minimum of 500,000 children to sailing and windsurfing in the UK; with more than 10% of them, becoming regular participants.

We want more young people to be able to join in the fun of sailing and windsurfing and take up the opportunities to stay involved in our sports. To find out more about OnBoard visit www.ruob.co.uk

RYA Champion Clubs

The RYA Champion Club Programme accredits and supports those clubs that have made a commitment to put the development of Junior Racing at the forefront of club activity. They are safe and effective places to develop your skills and there will almost certainly be one in your area. Team15 clubs encompass the same values but focus on the windsurfing rather than dinghy sailing.

The process is run by the RYA High Performance Managers. All details are listed in the RYA Website.

A Champion Club is required to:
- Provide a structured Junior Race Training Programme
- Guide their promising youngsters into the recognised youth classes following their period in a junior class.
- Have sufficient numbers of a recognised junior class of boat (members or club owned), equipment and qualified personnel to achieve the aims of partnership.

The Duke of Edinburgh's Award

The RYA is recognised as a National Operating Authority for The Duke of Edinburgh's Award. The DofE is a voluntary, non-competitive programme of activities for anyone aged 14 to 24, giving the opportunity to experience new activities or develop existing skills.

There are three progressive levels of programmes which, when successfully completed, lead to a Bronze, Silver or Gold Award.

Doing your DofE

Achieving a DofE Award can be made an adventure from beginning to end. Within an RYA club or training centre, there are already so many activities young people could take part in which can count towards their DofE. These could range from:

- Volunteering: Helping out at your local Training Centre, club or Team15 night on a regular basis, this could be as an assistant, in the kitchen or maybe even on the committee!
- Physical: Regularly taking part in Sailing or windsurfing activity, why not set yourself a goal to gain a certain certificate in the RYA National Sailing or Windsurfing scheme or maybe participate in regular club racing.
- Skill: All about developing your skills, whether practical, social or personal. You may choose to sharpen up your powerboating, learn a new skill such as boat repair work, become an instructor or perhaps increase your theory knowledge and learn all about meteorology!
- Residential and Expedition: You may never have been away from home before, let alone using your board or boat to go on an exciting adventure with friends, so now is the time!

	Volunteering	Physical	Skills	Expedition	Residential
Bronze (14+ Years)	3 months	3 months	3 months	Plan, train for and undertake a 2 day, 1 night expedition	
	All participants must undertake a further 3 months in the Volunteering, Physical or Skills sections				
Silver (15 + years)	6 months	Once section for 6 months and the other section for 3 months		Plan, train for and undertake a 3 day, 2 night expedition	
	Direct entrants must undertake a further 6 months in either the Volunteering or the longer of the Physical or Skills sections.				
Gold (16+ years)	12 months	One section for 12 months and the other section for 6 months		Plan, train for and undertake a 4 day, 3 night expedition	Undertake a shared activity in a residential setting away from home for 5 days and 4 nights.
	Direct entrants must undertake a further 6 months in either the Volunteering or the longer of the Physical or Skills sections.				

Getting involved as an Instructor, Coach or Trainer

There is a considerable amount of interaction between the participants and the adults who are supporting them, with specific DofE roles such as Centre Coordinators, Leaders, Supervisors and Assessors. If you are interested in helping, further information on these roles can be found by visiting the DofE website.

Further information can be found, explaining the opportunities available, on the DofE website www.dofe.org, and the RYA website www.rya.org.uk/go/dofe.

RYA Training Centre Recognition

RYA Training Centres

Only recognised centres can issue RYA certificates. These centres fall into three main categories:
- Centres open to the public.
- Clubs providing tuition for their members and prospective members.
- Organisations such as local education authorities, Scouts and HM Services, who are restricted to teaching their own groups or members.

RYA recognition is vested in the Principal and the site, and implies that certificated courses are run and that the remainder are closely associated with the aims of the National Windsurfing Scheme. The Principal is responsible for issuing RYA certificates and ensuring that the requirements of RYA recognition are maintained at all times.

An initial application fee is payable by all new recognised centres. Thereafter, an annual subscription is payable to the RYA, except in the case of centres who are already subscribing as affiliated clubs or associations. Full details of the recognition procedure and requirements are available from the RYA or by visiting our website. The Guidance Notes for the inspection of RYA Training Centres contain further in-depth information and can be found on the website www.rya.org.uk.

Duty of Care

Instructors and Coaches must always remember that they are usually teaching relatively inexperienced sailors, who may not be able to make a sound assessment of the risks inherent in the sport. Instructors and particularly Senior Instructors should not hesitate to make prudent decisions in unfavourable conditions to ensure the safety of the students in their care.

Instructor Health Declaration

RYA Instructors and Coaches must declare any medical condition which might affect their duty of care as an instructor. They also undertake to inform the RYA of any relevant change in their medical situation after qualifying. The RYA reserves the right to withhold or suspend qualification from anyone who is considered unlikely to fulfil this requirement.

Student Health Declaration

In order that they are informed as to any additional risk to students, RYA training centres are strongly advised to include a health declaration in their booking forms. The Principal/Chief Instructor must pass on such information to the individual instructor responsible for the student. The declaration should say that the student is, to the best of their knowledge, not suffering from epilepsy, disability, giddy spells, asthma, angina or other heart condition, and is fit to participate in the course. It should be signed and dated by the student and include details of any medical conditions or injuries and medication being taken. If there is doubt as to someone's fitness to take part, medical advice may be sought.

Swimmers

It is recommended that all those participating in the sport of sailing should be able to swim. No minimum level swimming ability is stipulated, but students should be able to demonstrate water confidence. It is essential that the instructor in charge of a course knows if any course members are non-swimmers. Non-swimmers may be required to wear life jackets instead of buoyancy aids.

Choosing the Right Simulator

A windsurfing simulator is a requirement of RYA recognition and one of the many aids available to you when teaching windsurfing. It is not the essence of the activity but, if used well, can be very effective for the initial introduction and for further coaching at all levels. More details can be found on the RYA website.

Basic Simulators

Used for teaching RYA Start Windsurfing, basic simulators should preferably have the following characteristics:

- Low to the ground.
- Stable base.
- Solid assembly.
- Damping system.
- Realistic board.
- Suitable rig.
- Mobility (if you need to move it).
- Clear wind location.
- Sufficient space around it.

Basic Stance or 'Funboard' Simulators

Necessity when teaching intermediate and advanced levels of the syllabus. The design should be sufficient for teaching techniques such as harness work, footstraps and the coaching system Fastfwd.

- Familiarity is key, so a modern, durable board similar to the one students will be using on the water is the best option.
- Lack of sheltered space often dictates that a rig without a sail is used. However, when possible you should use a small fully-battened rig.
- A pulley system such as a length of shock cord made into several loops with shackles on each end and a webbing adjustment. A safety leash to which is fitted a three point:
  1. From the main structure, 2. Half way along the pulley system and, if possible,
  3. On to the boom.
- The board should be placed on a soft surface or welded structure, in a position that allows the student to face the instructor (looking upwind), should also be easily changed to enable a beam to a broad reach.
- The wind can be made changeable by the pulley system (as described above) adjusted depending on wind strength, direction and the size of the student.

Transitions Simulator

A useful simulator and easy to construct – it's just a board with a rig in a clear area. Placing a mat or board bag under the board will enable the simulator to be manoeuvred through all points of sail as the transition is demonstrated or practised.

Safeguarding and Child Protection

Introduction

RYA Recognised Training Centres are required to have a formal child protection policy which is checked as part of their annual inspection. Your organisation is therefore strongly advised to take the following steps.

Adopt a policy statement that defines the organisation's commitment to providing a safe environment for children.

Produce a simple code of practice and procedures governing how the organisation runs.

The RYA publishes guidelines to help clubs, training centres and instructors to enable children and vulnerable adults to enjoy the sports of sailing, windsurfing and power boating in all their forms, in a safe environment. They can be copied or adapted to meet the requirements of the organisation. The document and other best practice guidance can be downloaded from the RYA's website www.rya.org.uk/go/childprotection.

The RYA Policy Statement on Child Protection is as follows:

As defined in the Children Act 1989, for the purposes of this policy anyone under the age of 18 should be considered as a child. The policy also applies to vulnerable adults.

It is the policy of the RYA to safeguard children and young people taking part in boating from physical, sexual or emotional harm. The RYA will take all reasonable steps to ensure that, through appropriate procedures and training, children participating in RYA activities do so in a safe environment. We recognise that the safety and welfare of the child is paramount and that all children, whatever their age, gender, disability, culture, ethnic origin, colour, religion or belief, social status or sexual identity, have a right to protection from abuse.

The RYA actively seeks to:

- Create a safe and welcoming environment, both on and off the water, where children can have fun and develop their skills and confidence.
- Support and encourage recognised training centres, affiliated clubs and class associations to implement similar policies.
- Recognise that safeguarding children is the responsibility of everyone, not just those who work with children.
- Ensure that RYA-organised training and events are run to the highest possible safety standards.
- Be prepared to review its ways of working to incorporate best practice.

We will:

- Treat all children with respect and celebrate their achievements.
- Carefully recruit and select all employees, contractors and volunteers.
- Respond swiftly and appropriately to all complaints and concerns about poor practice or suspected or actual child abuse.

This policy relates to all employees, contractors and volunteers who work with children or vulnerable adults in the course of their RYA duties. It will be kept under periodic review. All relevant concerns, allegations, complaints and their outcome should be notified to the RYA Child Protection Co-ordinator.

NOTE FOR PRINCIPALS – Good Recruitment Practice

If a good recruitment policy is adopted, and the issue of child protection covered in the organisation's risk assessment and operating procedures, both children and adults should be adequately protected. Potential abusers have difficulty operating in a well-run organisation. All applications, whether for paid or voluntary work, should be subject to an appropriate level of scrutiny. The level of checking you carry out should be proportionate to the role and the level of risk involved. The risk may be higher if the person will be in regular contact with the same child or children, in sole charge of children with no parents or other adults present, and/or in a role involving authority and trust, such as an instructor or coach.

The organisation should agree a clear policy and apply it fairly and consistently. Consider:

- **Who to check**
- **The level of check** to be conducted for each category
    - References.
    - Self-disclosure.
    - Enhanced Criminal Records Disclosure (and Barred List Check, if appropriate), or PVG Scheme Membership (Scotland).

Criminal Records Disclosures

Organisations affiliated to or recognised by the RYA can access the Disclosure process through the RYA. The procedure varies according to the home country and legal jurisdiction in which your organisation is located. Full up to date information is available from the RYA website, or contact the RYA's Safeguarding Co-ordinator.

GOOD PRACTICE GUIDELINES

Culture

It is important to develop a culture within your organisation where both children and adults feel able to raise concerns, knowing that they will be taken seriously, treated confidentially and will not make the situation worse for themselves or others. Some children may be more vulnerable to abuse or find it more difficult to express their concerns. For example, a disabled child who relies on a carer to help them get changed may worry that they won't be able to sail any more if they report the carer. A child who has experienced racism may find it difficult to trust an adult from a different ethnic background.

Minimising risk

Plan the work of the organisation and promote good practice to minimise situations where adults are working unobserved or could take advantage of their position of trust. Good practice protects everyone – children, volunteers and staff.

These common sense guidelines should be available to everyone within your organisation.
- Avoid spending any significant time working with children in isolation.
- Do not take children alone in a car, however short the journey.
- Do not take children to your home as part of your organisation's activity.
- Where any of these are unavoidable, ensure that they only occur with the full knowledge and consent of someone in charge of the organisation or the child's parents.
- Design training programmes that are within the ability of the individual child.
- If a child is having difficulty with a wetsuit or buoyancy aid, ask them to ask a friend to help if at all possible.
- If you do have to help a child, make sure you are in full view of others, preferably another adult.

You should never:

- Engage in rough, physical or sexually provocative games.
- Allow or engage in inappropriate touching of any form.
- Allow children to use inappropriate language unchallenged, or use such language yourself when with children.
- Make sexually suggestive comments to a child, even in fun.
- Fail to respond to an allegation made by a child – always act.
- Do things of a personal nature that children can do for themselves.

It may sometimes be necessary to do things of a personal nature for children, particularly if they are very young or disabled. These tasks should only be carried out with the full understanding and consent of both the child (where possible) and their parents/carers. In an emergency situation which requires this type of help, parents should be fully informed. In such situations it is important to ensure that any adult present is sensitive to the child and undertakes personal care tasks with the utmost discretion.

Responsibilities of Staff and Volunteers
Staff or volunteers should be given clear roles and responsibilities. They should be aware of your organisation's child protection policy and procedures and be given guidelines on:
- Following good practice.
- Recognising signs of abuse (see RYA Guidelines).

Identifying Child Abuse
The following brief notes provide a guide to help you identify signs of possible abuse and know what action to take in such cases. The RYA Safeguarding and Child Protection Guidelines on the RYA website cover the subject more fully.

Forms of Abuse
Abuse and neglect are forms of maltreatment of a child. Somebody may abuse or neglect a child by inflicting harm, or by failing to act to prevent harm. Children may be abused in a family or in an institutional or community setting, by those known to them or, more rarely, by a stranger. They may be abused by an adult or adults, or another child or children.

Physical abuse may involve adults or other children causing physical harm:
- by hitting, shaking, squeezing, biting or burning, giving children alcohol, inappropriate drugs or poison, attempting to suffocate or drown children
- in sport situations, physical abuse might also occur when the nature and intensity of training exceeds the capacity of the child's immature and growing body.

Neglect is the persistent failure to meet a child's basic physical and/or psychological needs, likely to result in the serious impairment of the child's health or development.
- neglect in a windsurfing situation might occur if an instructor or coach fails to ensure that children are safe, or exposes them to undue cold or risk of injury.

Sexual abuse. Sexual abuse involves an individual forcing or enticing a child or young person to take part in sexual activities, whether or not the child is aware of what is happening, to meet their own sexual needs. The activities may involve:

- actual physical contact or encouraging children to behave in sexually inappropriate ways
- showing children pornographic books, photographs, videos or online images or taking pictures of children for pornographic purposes
- sport situations which involve physical contact (eg. supporting or guiding children) could potentially create situations where sexual abuse may go unnoticed. Abusive situations may also occur if adults misuse their power over young people.

Emotional abuse is the persistent emotional maltreatment of a child such as to cause severe and persistent adverse effects on the child's emotional development.

- emotional abuse in sport might include situations where parents or coaches subject children to constant criticism, bullying or pressure to perform at a level that the child cannot realistically be expected to achieve.

Some level of emotional abuse is involved in all types of maltreatment of a child.

Bullying (including cyberbullying) may be seen as deliberately hurtful behaviour, usually repeated or sustained over a period of time, where it is difficult for those being bullied to defend themselves. The bully may often be another young person. Although anyone can be the target of bullying, victims are typically shy, sensitive and perhaps anxious or insecure. Sometimes they are singled out for physical reasons – being overweight, physically small, having a disability or belonging to a different race, faith or culture.

Recognising Signs of Possible Abuse

It is not always easy, even for the most experienced carers, to spot when a child has been abused. However, some of the more typical symptoms which should trigger your suspicions would include:

- Unexplained or suspicious injuries such as bruising, cuts or burns, particularly if situated on a part of the body not normally prone to such injuries.
- Sexually explicit language or actions.
- A sudden change in behaviour (eg. becoming very quiet, withdrawn or displaying sudden outbursts of temper).
- The child describes what appears to be an abusive act involving him/her.
- A change observed over a long period of time (eg. the child losing weight or becoming increasingly dirty or unkempt).
- A general distrust and avoidance of adults, especially those with whom a close relationship would be expected.
- An unexpected reaction to normal physical contact.
- Difficulty in making friends or abnormal restrictions on socialising with others.

It is important to note that a child could be displaying some or all of these signs, or behaving in a way which is worrying, without this necessarily meaning that the child is being abused. Similarly, there may not be any signs, but you may just feel that something is wrong.

Listening to the Child
Children may confide in adults they trust, in a place where they feel at ease.

Always:

- Stay calm – ensure that the child is safe and feels safe.
- Show and tell the child that you are taking what he/she says seriously.
- Reassure that child and stress that he/she is not to blame.
- Be careful about physical contact, it may not be what the child wants.
- Be honest, explain that you will have to tell someone else to help stop the alleged abuse.
- Make a record of what the child has said as soon as possible after the event.
- Follow your organisation's child protection procedures.

Never:

- Rush into actions that may be inappropriate.
- Make promises you cannot keep (eg. you won't tell anyone).
- Ask more questions than are necessary for you to be sure that you need to act.
- Take sole responsibility – consult someone else (ideally the designated Child Protection/ Welfare Officer or the person in charge or someone you can trust) so that you can begin to protect the child and gain support for yourself.

What to do if you are concerned about a child or about the behaviour of a member of staff:

A complaint, concern or allegation may come from a number of sources: a child, their parents or someone within your organisation. It may involve the behaviour of one of your volunteers, employees, or an incident relating to the child at home or at school. Allegations can range from mild verbal bullying to physical or sexual abuse.

If you have noticed a change in the child's behaviour, first talk to the parents or carers. It may be that something has occurred, such as a bereavement, which has caused the child to be unhappy. However if there are concerns about sexual abuse or violence in the home, talking to the parents or carers might put the child at greater risk.

It is NOT your responsibility to investigate further; however, it is your responsibility to act on your concerns and report them to the organisation's Child Protection/Welfare Officer or person in charge, who will make the decision to contact Children's Services or the Police and report to the RYA Safeguarding Co-ordinator. There are simple flow diagrams in the RYA Guidelines that take you through the actions to be taken.

If you have concerns regarding the behaviour of a member of staff or volunteer, inform the organisation's designated Child Protection/Welfare Officer or the person in charge, who should follow the RYA's procedures. It may become necessary for the member of staff to be temporarily suspended while an investigation takes place.

It is important to understand that a member of staff reporting suspicions of child abuse, particularly by a colleague, may undergo a very high degree of stress, including feelings of guilt for having reported the matter. It is therefore very important to ensure that appropriate counselling and support is available for staff.

RYA Equality Policy

Policy Statement

The RYA is committed to the principle of equality of opportunity and aims to ensure that all present and potential participants, members, instructors, coaches, competitors, officials, volunteers and employees are treated fairly and on an equal basis, irrespective of sex, age, disability, race, colour, religion or belief, sexual orientation, pregnancy and maternity, marriage and civil partnerships, gender reassignment or social status.

Objectives

- To make boating an activity that is genuinely open to anyone who wishes to take part.
- To provide the framework for everyone to enjoy the sport, in whatever capacity and to whatever level the individual desires.
- To ensure that the RYA's services, including training schemes, are accessible to all, including those who have been under-represented in the past.

Implementation

- The RYA encourages its affiliated clubs and organisations and its recognised training centres to adopt a similar policy, so that they are seen as friendly, welcoming and open to all.
- Appointments to voluntary or paid positions with the RYA will be made on the basis of an individual's knowledge, skills and experience and the competences required for the role.
- The RYA will relax regulations in relation to RYA training schemes which may inhibit the performance of candidates with special needs, provided that the standard, quality and integrity of schemes and assessments are not compromised.
- The RYA reserves the right to discipline any of its members or employees who practise any form of discrimination in breach of this policy.
- The effectiveness of this policy will be monitored and evaluated on an ongoing basis.

Appeals Procedure

All RYA qualified instructors and trainers are required to treat students and candidates with respect and fairness.

All assessments in the use of boats and their equipment have implications for the safety of participants. It is therefore essential that candidates be given a thorough and searching assessment. It would be dangerous to the candidate and anyone whom they subsequently teach if a trainer erred on the side of leniency in awarding a certificate. There must never be any question of relaxing the standards required for an award.

Realistic Aims

In some cases, it becomes clear to the trainer at an early stage in the assessment process that the candidate has been over-ambitious in their choice of award. In such instances the trainer should discuss the situation with the candidate and agree revised achievable aims.

Grounds for Appeal

A candidate has grounds for appeal if he or she believes that:

- They have not been given a reasonable opportunity to demonstrate their competence.
- The person carrying out the assessment has placed them under undue or unfair pressure.
- The trainer has reached the wrong conclusion on the basis of the outcome of the candidate's performance in the assessment.

The Procedure

The candidate should first raise the concern with the trainer to see if the matter can be amicably resolved. If it is inappropriate to consult the trainer no amicable solution can be reached, so the candidate should within 20 working days of the assessment appeal in writing to the RYA Chief Windsurfing Instructor. The letter of appeal should contain the following:

- Full details of the assessment – when, where, involving whom etc.
- The nature of the appeal.
- Any supporting documentation relating to the assessment – outcome, action plans, reports etc.

On receipt of an appeal, an investigaton will commence. Following investigation, the candidate will be informed of the outcome, which will be one of the following:

- The original decision confirmed.
- The assessment is to be carried out again by the same or a different trainer.
- The original decision overturned and the assessment judged to be adequate.

If the candidate is still unhappy about the decision, they can appeal against the outcome to the RYA Training Committee.

Avoiding Complaints

Most complaints occur due to a lack of communication between the candidate and the instructor or training centre.

Large centres usually have separate staff selling and marketing the courses to those actually delivering them. A lack of specialist knowledge can lead to incorrect information being provided at the booking enquiry. In smaller centres this is less likely to happen as initial enquiries and bookings are often dealt with by instructors or staff with a good knowledge of the courses and their suitability.

Staff booking candidates onto courses should understand the selling points, the content and any prerequisites candidates will need. This sounds straightforward, but a large number of complaints are due to the wrong information being given from the start, leading to incorrect or unrealistic expectations from candidates.

To help clear any confusion, consider producing a set of concise instructions and advice on all the courses on offer, content, structure and pre-course requirements. Taking a close look at course feedback can also help identify potential problems and increase customer service. The RYA adult and youth windsurfing schemes are progressive courses and clinics, designed to be delivered in a flexible and accessible way. Adults, particularly, tend to research the course they will be attending in some depth. They therefore expect to receive the tuition they have paid for, as set out in the RYA syllabus (see the appropriate RYA Logbook).

Before and during the course, talk through the programme with candidates letting them know the course is subject to change depending on the group's ability and progress. Ensure their aims are realistic and attainable, and keep them informed on their progress throughout. Try to identify anyone who is struggling early and ensure they continue to feel part of the group. A competent instructor with good personal skills will be able to use tact and diplomacy to create an environment in which everyone can progress.

Providing continual feedback throughout the course ensures candidates understand how they are doing and what is necessary to complete the course or clinic. If one is falling short of the required level for a certificate, continual feedback will make the end of the course easier all round. Rather than having a dissatisfied candidate on your hands who is simply told they have failed, they will be clear about how they can improve and the standard required to obtain the certificate.

Remember, not every course can be perfect. No matter how hard you try, you could come across a candidate who is a "born complainer". As long as you ensure that everyone is clear about the aims and scope of the course from start right to finish, you should be able to keep complaints to the minimum. If a customer does complain, it is important that the Principal or Chief Instructor deals with it personally and quickly, remaining as impartial as possible and to research the allegations carefully ensuring the facts are obtained, before deciding on the best resolution.

RYA National Windsurfing Scheme

The National Windsurfing Scheme

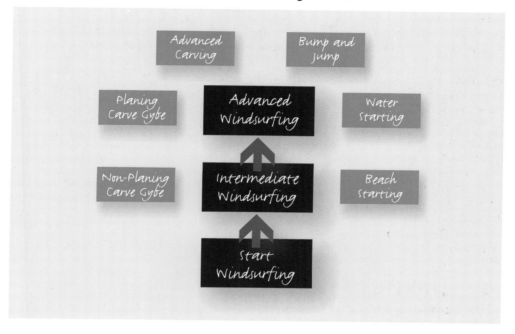

Within our National Scheme there are core courses (Start, Intermediate and Advanced), with additional clinics concentrating on key skills (gybing, beachstarting and waterstarting etc). This also ensures a tailored approach to an individual's needs and teaching environment. The Youth Scheme directly relates to the National Scheme, providing ease of use and comparison. On completing Stage 4, your students should have the skill and ability to progress through the advanced courses and clinics of the National Scheme. For information on assessing ability and teaching the different levels of the National and Youth Windsurfing Schemes, refer to pages 64-67.

The Youth Windsurfing Scheme and its comparison to the National Scheme

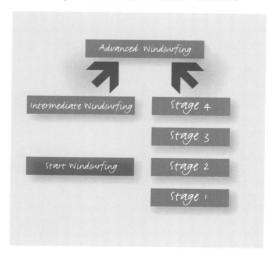

Who Teaches What?

RYA tuition at recognised training centres must comply with the appropriate tuition and safety boat guidelines.

It is the responsibility of the Principal or Chief Instructor to ensure instructors are teaching to RYA standards, this includes good teaching methods delivered on appropriate equipment with suitable student/instructor ratios, as outlined in the appropriate RYA publications.

Unless dispensation is granted by RYA HQ, all proficiency courses should be run with no more than six students to each instructor.

A RYA centre is required to have a RYA Senior Instructor to supervise tuition and maintain recognition for dinghy sailing and windsurfing. Further details are available within RYA Organisation (page 5) and included in the Guidance Notes which are available on www.rya.org.uk.

RYA Teaching Ratios

Instructor Qualifications	can teach National Scheme course	can teach Youth Scheme course	Ratio
Start Windsurfing Instructor	Start Windsurfing	Stage 1 and 2	1:6
Intermediate Instructor (Non Planing)	Intermediate (Non Planing)	Stage 1 to 3	1:6
Intermediate Instructor (Planing)	Intermediate (Planing)	Stage 1 to 4	1:6
Advanced Instructor	Advanced	Stage 1 to 4	1:6
Advanced Instructor (Plus)	Advanced (Plus)	Stage 1 to 4	1:6
Senior Instructor	Supervisory qualification		
RYA Trainer Qualifications			
RYA Start Trainer	Start Windsurfing and Senior Instructor Courses	All	1:8
RYA Intermediate Trainer	Start, Intermediate and Senior Instructor Courses	All	1:8
RYA Advanced Trainer	Start, Intermediate, Advanced and Senior Instructor Courses	All	1:8
RYA Racing Qualifications			
Racing Instructor	N/A	Start Racing	
Racing Coach Level 2 (Club Racing Coach)	N/A	Start and Intermediate Racing (Advanced where appropriate)	
Racing Coach Level 3 (Class Racing Coach)	N/A	Start, Intermediate and Advanced Racing	

RYA Windsurfing Instructor Pathway

There are designated instructor pathways for both the training and racing schemes, each requiring different knowledge and experience.

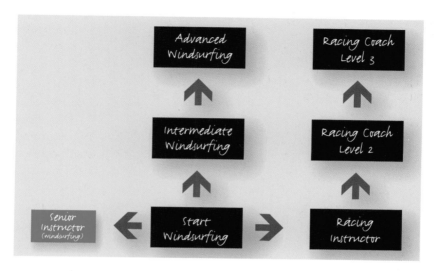

On successful completion of a RYA instructor course, the course trainer will submit your information to RYA Certification Department. Once processed an instructor certificate will be sent outlining the level of your instructor qualification, basic terms and the qualification expiry date. To RYA members the certificate administration is free of charge, for non members there is an administration fee, please ask your course trainer or contact the RYA direct for further information.

All windsurfing instructor qualifications are endorsed as either tidal or non tidal, depending on where the course or sailing assessment took place, and the appraisal of the course trainer. To change an instructor qualification from non-tidal to tidal, an assessment must be made by a trainer or suitably qualified instructor. The trainer will consider the instructor's capabilities on the water during instructing and personal sailing. Accompanying the Instructor Handbook are National Scheme publications.

RYA Publications available from the RYA webshop:

W33 – RYA Windsurfing Instructor Manual
W1 – RYA Youth Windsurfing Scheme
      Syllabus & Logbook
G47 – RYA National Windsurfing Scheme
      Syllabus & Logbook
G49 – RYA Start Windsurfing
G51 – RYA Intermediate Windsurfing
G52 – RYA Advanced Windsurfing

YR1 – RYA Racing Rules of Sailing
      2013–2016
YR7 – RYA Handy Guide to the Racing Rules
      2013–2016
Racing Instructor Manual Champion Club TV -
www.ryachampionclubtv.co.uk/
Windsurfing Race Training Exercises Manual
from the RYA website www.rya.org.uk.

RYA Windsurfing Instructor Training

The instructor pathway in training and racing is progressive, with clear steps helping you to progress through the levels as your coaching advances and your personal skills improve. The table below outlines the qualification ladder and associated information:

RYA Instructor Qualifications	Run By	Moderator	Length of Course	Course Ratio
Assistant Instructor	Senior Instructor	N/A	Centre specific	Centre specific
Start Instructor	RYA Start Trainer or above	Moderated by a trainer	5 days (last day is a Moderation)	1:8
Intermediate Instructor	RYA Intermediate Trainer or above	None	4 days	1:8
Advanced Instructor	RYA Advanced Trainer or above	None	4 days	1:8
Senior Instructor	RYA Trainer	None	4 days	Minimum of 6 candidates
RYA Racing Qualifications				
Racing Instructor	RYA Trainer (by appointment) or Racing Tutor	None	2 days or assessment on a Start Instructor Course	1:8
Racing Coach Level 2	Racing Tutor	None	2 days	1:6
Racing Coach Level 3	RYA HQ	None	2 weekends, plus additional work	2:12

The following information provides you with a general description of each RYA windsurfing qualification, course information and content, assessments that take place and any prerequisites needed prior to attending the course. Further information can be found on the RYA Website.

Assistant Instructor

General Description
This course is designed to offer an introductory level to coaching windsurfing or dinghy sailing. It is for those intending to qualify as an RYA Instructor and is certified by the Centre Principal or nominated Chief Instructor.

Eligibility
The Assistant Windsurfing instructor is a competent windsurfer who works under the supervision of a fully qualified instructor at all times. Candidates must hold the minimum of an Intermediate Non-Planing Personal Certificate (including the beachstarting and non-planing carve gybe clinics), they are not qualified to use a powerboat unless they hold the RYA Powerboat Level 2 certificate.

Course Information and Content
Training is provided by the Centre Principal or nominated Chief Instructor who holds a Senior Instructor qualification. It may be run as a specific Assistant Instructor course over about 20 hours or provided on a one-to-one basis over a longer period as on-the-job training. As the Assistant Instructor qualification is centre specific, the training will be related directly to the work of that particular centre.

Assessment
Candidates will be assessed on their practical teaching ability with beginners. Successful candidates will have their logbook signed and be awarded an RYA Assistant Instructor Certificate by their Principal. This certificate is only valid at that centre for five years, although the certificate can be re-issued by the Centre Principal. During the five years it is recommended that candidates look towards training as a fully qualified RYA instructor.

Start Windsurfing Instructor

General Description

A Start Windsurfing Instructor is a competent windsurfer trained to teach and assess the Start Windsurfing syllabus of the RYA National Windsurfing Scheme and Stage 1 and 2 of the Youth Scheme.

Start instructors are confident windsurfers capable of teaching the basic skills of windsurfing in light to medium winds. During the course, candidates will be assessed on their competence to teach both adults and children to the level of RYA Start Windsurfing and Youth Stage 1 and 2.

Course Prerequisites

- Minimum age: 16.
- Candidates must hold an Intermediate non-planing personal certificate (including the beachstarting and non-planing carve gybe clinics).
- RYA Powerboat Level 2 certificate.
- A valid RYA First Aid Certificate, or another acceptable first aid qualification detailed on the RYA website (www.rya.org.uk/go/firstaidcertificates).
- RYA membership.

Course Information and Content

Duration: 5 days

Course Content

During the Start Windsurfing course a number of aspects will be covered to ensure the candidate's knowledge to teach under the supervision of a Senior Instructor. Below are just some of the areas covered:

- The RYA Schemes.
- The Start Windsurfing teaching method (on water, self rescue techniques, ashore).
- Theoretical knowledge.
- Presentation techniques.
- Course management.
- Powerboat rescue techniques.
- Personal skills and sailing assessment (*).
- Equipment and Simulators.

*During the course a sailing assessment may be carried out covering the basic skills and techniques an instructor would be expected to show, such as stopping and starting under control, turning on the spot, tacking and gybing; passing this assessment is a requirement of the qualification, further details can be found on page 138.

Assessment

The Start Windsurfing course runs over five days, with the final day moderated by an external trainer who has not been involved in, or associated with, the training course. During the moderation candidates may be required to demonstrate confident ability in any of the following areas:

- Delivery of on and off water sessions.
- Preparation, management and structure of the sessions.
- Theoretical knowledge.
- Sailing ability.

Intermediate Windsurfing Instructor

General Description
An Intermediate Windsurfing Instructor is a confident, experienced windsurfer with wide theoretical knowledge. They are trained to teach and assess the Start and Intermediate non-planing and/or planing windsurfing courses of the RYA National Windsurfing Schemes and Stage 1 to 4 of the Youth schemes, under the supervision of a RYA Senior Instructor.

The Intermediate course can be assessed in two competencies: non-planing and planing. It is the first instructor course to incorporate the Fastfwd coaching model. Candidates will cover teaching of all clinics incorporated within the Intermediate syllabus during the course.

Course Prerequisites
- Minimum age: 16.
- RYA Start Windsurfing Instructor, with evidence of 50 hours logged as a Start Windsurfing Instructor at RYA training centre.
- Candidates must hold an Intermediate planing personal sailing certificate and the beachstarting and non-planing carve gybe clinics.
- Candidates must hold an Advanced personal sailing certificate with waterstart and carve gybe clinics.
- RYA Powerboat level 2 certificate.
- A valid RYA First Aid Certificate, or another acceptable first aid qualification detailed on the RYA website (www.rya.org.uk/go/firstaidcertificates).

Course Information and Content
Duration: 4 days
Course Content
- The RYA Schemes.
- Delivery of the Intermediate teaching method using Fastfwd, on water and ashore.
- Self rescue techniques.
- Presentation techniques and theoretical knowledge.
- The development of personal sailing skills.
- Powerboat rescue techniques.
- Course management.
- Equipment.
- Simulators.

Assessment
There is no moderation during the Intermediate Instructor Course due to candidates being continually assessed by the course trainer. Candidates will be required to demonstrate confident ability in the following areas:
- Delivery of on water and on shore sessions.
- Preparation, management and structure of the sessions.
- Theoretical knowledge.
- Sailing ability.

Advanced Windsurfing Instructor

General Description

The RYA Advanced Instructor qualification is the highest windsurfing instructor award. An Instructor of this level is an experienced and very competent instructor, with excellent personal sailing ability and extensive theoretical knowledge. Instructors qualified to this level are able to teach all levels of the RYA National and Youth Scheme, under the supervision of a RYA Senior Instructor.

The Advanced course has a clinic-based approach, appealing to a wider spectrum of windsurfers. As with the Intermediate Course, Advanced can be assessed in two competencies depending upon the candidate's level of personal sailing and coaching ability – Advanced and Advanced Plus. The outcome is decided by the course trainer and determines which clinics the instructor is eligible to teach.

Course Prerequisites

- Minimum age: 18.
- Minimum personal ability of the Advanced certificate.
- RYA Intermediate planing instructor, with evidence of 100 hours logged.
- RYA Powerboat Level 2 certificate.
- A valid RYA First Aid Certificate, or another acceptable first aid qualification detailed on the RYA website (www.rya.org.uk/go/firstaidcertificates).

Course Information and Content

Course duration: 5 days

Course Content

- The RYA Schemes.
- Delivery of the Advanced teaching method using Fastfwd, on water and ashore.
- Self rescue and powerboat rescue techniques.
- Presentation techniques and theoretical knowledge.
- The development of personal sailing skills.
- Course management.
- Equipment and simulators.

On successful completion of the course, the trainer will submit your information to the RYA Certification Department. An Instructor Certificate will be sent to you outlining the level of qualification you hold, basic terms and the qualification expiry date. For RYA members the certificate administration is free of charge, for non members there is an administration fee. Contact the RYA for current fees.

Assessment

There is no moderation during the Advanced Instructor Course as candidates are continually assessed by the course trainer. Candidates will be required to demonstrate confident ability in the following areas:

- Delivery of on water and on shore sessions.
- Preparation, management and structure of the sessions.
- Theoretical knowledge.
- Sailing ability.

Senior Windsurfing Instructor

As an instructor reading the following information you may feel you are already fulfilling the roles required of a RYA Senior Instructor, or you need further knowledge and experience.

To attend a RYA Senior Instructor Course it is necessary to log a required amount of time teaching at RYA Training Centres and obtain a nomination from your Principal/Chief Instructor (see page 150). Your Principal or Chief Instructor will be able to assist in your decision regarding attending the course. Further information about the course and its content can be found on the RYA website and in the Senior Instructor Workbook.

RYA Senior Instructors need to be responsible, and be resourceful at solving the problems that will undoubtedly arise. You must direct, assist and support the work of instructors, and in particular, be there when they need advice. If you are unsure if you are ready to fulfil the role, the self assessment questionnaire on the RYA website will help, as will thinking through the scenarios below.

1 One of my students is learning far more quickly that the others. What do I do?
2 It's blowing Force 5 out there. What do I do? (day two of a Start course!).
3 What should I do with my hands when I'm lecturing?
4 You've asked me to cover for Rob while he's away. How do I know what his students have covered so far? (third day of an Intermediate course).
5 How do I tell when my students are ready to move on to the next level of the syllabus?
6 Bob and Hazel say they're too old to take part in some of the exercises I have planned. What do I tell them?
7 What do I do if three of my group get tired all at once and are unable to return to shore?
8 Why should I shave? (From a 22-year-old male instructor).
9 Why should I bother with the killcord on the outboard? It only gets in the way.
10 How do I teach Susie to windsurf? She's hearing impaired.

Eligibility
- Minimum age: 18.
- RYA Start Windsurfing Instructor, with evidence of two seasons full-time instructing.
- Recommendation by a Principal of a recognised training centre, (see page 150).
- A valid RYA First Aid Certificate, or another acceptable first aid qualification detailed on the RYA website (www.rya.org.uk/go/firstaidcertificates).
- RYA Safety Boat certificate.

Course Information and Content
Duration: 4 days, staffed by two or more RYA Windsurfing Trainers (depending on course numbers)

Assessment
The assessment will be continuous throughout the course.

Course Content

A Senior Instructor is not expected to have the answers to every eventuality. But during the Senior Instructor course the trainers will set up scenarios and discussion workshops to encourage the course group to learn from each others' experiences, and investigate new solutions that may never have been experienced.

Candidates will be asked to demonstrate their sailing ability to at least the standard of an RYA Start Windsurfing Instructor combined with a confident understanding of the National and Youth Windsurfing Schemes.

Daily Organisation

Every course has four elements: the students, the instructors, the equipment/teaching facilities and the syllabus. A Senior Instructor must ensure they all fit together harmoniously.

Session Planning

A good Senior Instructor should be able to plan, organise and run practical and shore based sessions, in addition to assisting their instructors in doing the same. For further details on session planning please see pages 73-75.

Course Material

The following material is required and downloadable from the RYA website:
- Senior Instructor Workbook, to be completed prior to course.
- W4a Start Windsurfing Method.
- Intermediate Coaching notes.
- Advanced Coaching notes.

Required Publications

National Windsurfing Scheme Logbooks:
- W1 – RYA Youth Windsurfing Scheme Syllabus & Logbook.
- G47 – RYA National Windsurfing Scheme Syllabus & Logbook.

Handbooks

- G49 – RYA Start Windsurfing.
- G51 – RYA Intermediate Windsurfing.
- G52 – RYA Advanced Windsurfing.
- W33 – RYA Windsurfing Instructor Manual.

Becoming an RYA Windsurfing Trainer

General Description
Teaching within the RYA's National schemes is progressive. You can develop your skills and qualifications by taking the next step on the ladder, working towards either the Senior Instructor level or furthering your coaching skills with the Advanced Instructor course, or perhaps both.

If you enjoy developing people's skills, are seen as a role model and want to put something back into the scheme, becoming a trainer may be for you. The RYA requires trainers with sensitivity to individuals' needs, in addition to being a strong role model. Enthusiasm and a commitment to the RYA schemes are essential, as are having an approachable and friendly attitude.

RYA Windsurfing Trainers need to be competent, experienced windsurfers, with good teaching and coaching skills, motivational and leadership skills, a positive and enthusiastic approach, and good communicational skills. The role is broad and candidates must be willing to involve themselves in all aspects of the RYA National and Youth Windsurfing Schemes.

RYA Windsurfing Trainers are appointed annually and are required to attend an update at least every five years. Progression to RYA Intermediate and Advanced Trainers is via an application to RYA Training.

Eligibility
- An experienced windsurfing RYA Senior Instructor and Intermediate Planing Instructor, held for approximately three years or more.
- A valid RYA First Aid Certificate, or another acceptable first aid qualification detailed on the RYA website (www.rya.org.uk/go/firstaidcertificates).
- RYA Safety Boat Certificate.
- Nomination from your Regional Development Officer or RYA Training Headquarters if overseas.
- RYA membership.

Course Information and Content
The course consists of several parts:
1 Completion of an application – available via your RDO or RYA Training.
2 Two day selection.
3 Apprenticeship and/or action plan.
4 Five Day Trainer's Course.

Selection Course

Duration: 2 days

The course gives guidance to candidates on their readiness for the role and preparation for the Training Course. All candidates will receive an action plan which must be completed prior to attending the Trainers Course.

The Trainers Course

Duration: 5 days

Designed to deliver information and guidance on the main roles, after which candidates must assist experienced Trainers and then run their own instructor course, which will be moderated. Successful candidates will be appointed as RYA Start Windsurfing Trainers.

Candidates attending the Trainers course should be able to:

- Demonstrate and teach any part of the National Scheme up to and including the Intermediate syllabus and clinics.
- Windsurf competently on a range of equipment in a variety of conditions.
- Plan and manage a course involving sessions ashore and afloat.
- Give formal, informal presentations and lead discussions, including the use of visual aids, showing an ability to chair and discuss.

Racing Instructor

General Description

A RYA Racing Instructor qualification is an endorsement on an existing RYA Windsurfing Instructor qualification. A Racing Instructor is an experienced windsurfer who would like to get involved in setting up and running club level competition for adults or a Team15 club for children and teenagers. Personal competition experience is not essential though would be an advantage.

Eligibility

To qualify as a RYA Racing Instructor applicants should fulfil the following criteria:

- Have a practical understanding of running simple race training exercises.
- Have knowledge and understanding of the Team15 philosophy and the teaching principles behind the programme.
- Have knowledge of local/regional competition, Team15, RYA High Performance Manager and UKWA.
- Have knowledge and understanding of the RYA Junior and Youth equipment pathway and squad programme.

If the applicant has not fulfilled all of the above they can be given an action plan to take away and report back.

Course Information and Content

There are two routes to becoming a RYA Racing Instructor; which route is taken depends on whether the candidate has personal competition experience, or not.

- **Route 1** – available to windsurfers who have personal competition experience (windsurfing or dinghy sailing) wishing to take a RYA Windsurfing Instructor Qualification (Start Windsurfing Instructor or above).
- **Route 2** – available to Start Windsurfing Instructors (or above) who have no personal competition experience.

Route 1

Candidates will have competed at club or regional level (windsurfing or dinghy sailing) and have knowledge of competitive windsurfing.

As part of the relevant RYA Instructor Course candidates will look at the basics of running race training exercises and sessions.

Course Information and Content
RYA instructor course (Start Windsurfing Instructor or above)
Duration: 4-5 day course (depending on instructor course taken)

Course Prerequisites
Personal competition experience at club or regional level (windsurfing or dinghy sailing) plus prerequisites for the appropriate windsurfing instructor course (outlined on pages 24-26).

Assessment
Is carried out by the trainer during the 4-5 day course. Candidates may be assessed on any of the areas outlined in Eligibility (see page 33).

Route 2
This route is the only option available to candidates without personal competition experience (windsurfing or dinghy sailing). Candidates must already have qualified as a RYA Start Windsurfing Instructor.

The course looks at windsurfing competition in the UK and the opportunities available to children and adults. It runs through practical coaching sessions for delivering the RYA Start Racing syllabus and explains the philosophy and teaching principles behind the Team15 programme (further details can be found on page 5).

Course Information and Content
RYA Racing Instructor
Duration: 2 days

Course Prerequisites
Start Windsurfing Instructor

Assessment
Is continuous throughout the 2 day course, carried out by the RYA Racing Instructor Tutor. Candidates may be assessed on any of the areas outlined in Eligibility above.

Publications
- W3 – RYA Racing Instructor Manual
- W1 – RYA Youth Windsurfing Scheme Syllabus & Logbook
- YR1 – RYA Racing Rules of Sailing 2013–2016
- YR7 – RYA Handy Guide to the Racing Rules 2013–2016
- The RYA Youth Racing Programme Handbook

Racing Coach Level 2 Windsurfing

General Description

A qualified RYA Racing Coach Level 2 is an experienced windsurfer with personal knowledge of club and/or regional racing. They have a broad base of coaching skills and are able to deliver RYA Start, Intermediate Racing courses, and Advanced Racing where appropriate. They work at affiliated clubs or recognised training centres.

The Course is an intense weekend looking at the theory of coaching and applying it to a series of on the water exercises. Each candidate will be expected to run complete sessions including a brief, on the water exercises with feedback and debrief. The aim of the course is to provide candidates with a range of skills and techniques to coach racing to youths and adults.

Eligibility

- Appropriate racing experience (Club, Regional or National).
- Appropriate current racing knowledge (classes and pathways).
- RYA Powerboat Level 2 certificate.
- A valid RYA First Aid Certificate, or another acceptable first aid qualification detailed on the RYA website (www.rya.org.uk/go/firstaidcertificates).
- Minimum age: 16. RYA Racing Coaches aged under 18 should be supervised by an adult who is either a Senior Instructor or a Racing Coach Level 2 or above.
- Previous instructing experience is preferred but is not essential if the candidate has suitable alternative experience.

Course Information and Content

Duration: 2 days
Run by RYA Racing Coach Tutor

Application

Candidates should apply online at www.ryainteractive.org. High Performance Managers will assess all applications and the suitability of candidates and can answer any queries.

Revalidation

Racing Coaches are requested to revalidate every 5 years to ensure their continued effectiveness as a coach.

- Complete the Revalidation Form on the Racing Coaches section of the RYA website and send it to:
  Caroline Sullivan, Racing Department, RYA House, Ensign Way, Hamble, Southampton SO31 4YA

You also need to send a copy of:

- A valid First Aid certificate - to see if your first aid certificate is valid go to http://www.rya.org.uk/coursestraining/resources/Pages/Firstaidandmedical.aspx

Progression to Racing Coach Level 3 – Class Racing Coach, is via application to the RYA Racing Department

Methods of Instructing and Coaching

YOUR ROLE - INSTRUCTOR OR COACH

As a RYA Windsurfing Instructor you will need to adapt to the role of both instructor and coach. The role chosen at any time will depend on a number of factors:

- The type of session (practical or theory).
- The subject (new subject or developing existing skills).
- The teaching method (discussion, demonstration or student practice).
- The environment (ashore or afloat).
- Number of students.
- Where they are in the RYA Scheme.

Your role as an **instructor** is to help students learn by teaching them practical and theoretical aspects of the sport. It mostly involves explaining and demonstrating skills which are new to them.

However, **coaching** implies a shift towards helping students develop the skills they have already been taught. It may involve more observation, feedback and questioning to check their understanding of the skills.

A typical session might follow this simple model which shows how your role evolves from instructor to coach as your students progress through their course.

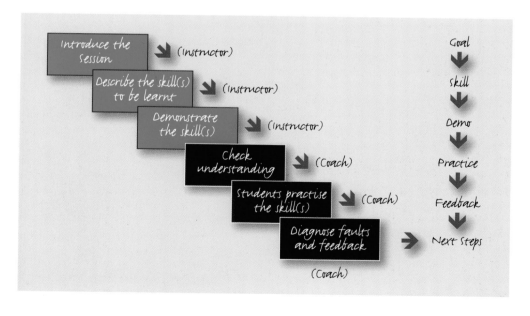

If you coach your students effectively their performance should improve and any problems that prevent them progressing can be solved.

Effective coaching needs:

- A mutual desire to coach/be coached.
- Empathy towards your students.
- Good communication between coach and student.
- A focus on goals.

There are main processes involved in coaching.

1. Communication
- Listening.
- Questioning.
- Responding.
- Giving feedback.

2. Influencing
- Increasing confidence and independence in your students.
- Positively reinforcing things done well.

3. Helping
- Expressing concern for, and empathy with students.
- Establishing support for students.
- Identifying students' needs and linking this to their goals.

Remember that we are communicating all the time. Our thoughts and emotions can often 'leak' out through verbal and non-verbal communication.

Coaches should therefore:

- Develop their verbal and non-verbal communication skills.
- Ensure they provide constructive feedback during sessions.
- Give students equal or appropriate attention.
- Ensure you listen to students, not just talk at them!

HELPING YOUR STUDENTS TO LEARN

Breaking Down the Activity

Windsurfing is a fun, practical and exciting sport and requires experimental learning – in other words, learning through doing. It helps to break it down into four stages:

- Run a structured activity or session.
- Review and discuss what happened during the session.
- Help your students learn and be sure what they know.
- Encourage students to apply their learning to future sessions.

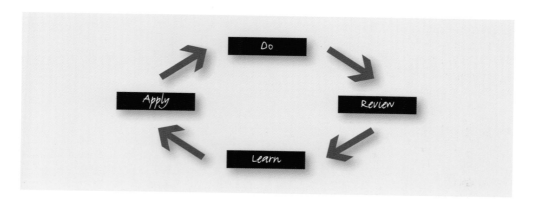

Throughout this process students need:
- Positive and constructive feedback.
- Time to reflect.
- Structured sessions that build on each other.

Exactly how you tackle these four stages can be determined by understanding how your students absorb information and learn new skills.

Absorbing Information

Not everyone sees and experiences the world in the same way. We take in information through our senses. VARK is an easy way to remember:
- Visual – eyes.
- Auditory – ears.
- Reading – reading and writing.
- Kinaesthetic – touch, feel and movement.

These senses are pathways to our brains. None of us use one pathway exclusively – there is a significant overlap between them, but your students are likely to have a preference:

Visual Preference

Visual preference students make up around 40 - 60% of the population. *Students relate well to written information, pictures and observation. Typically they will benefit from* sessions where they can observe skills and possibly take notes. In some cases, information won't seem real unless they have seen it written down. They will respond well to demonstrations both ashore and afloat, and a range of visual aids.

Auditory Learners

Auditory preference students make up about 10 - 30% of the population. Students relate well to the spoken word. They like to hear clear, verbal explanations of skills both afloat and ashore. Often written information will have little meaning until it has been heard, and it may help them if they read written information out loud. Auditory learners can be sophisticated speakers, and work in jobs which require this skill.

Reading Learners

Will prefer to look at the relevant RYA publications. They will usually ask what topic will be covered on the next session so they can read up and investigate beforehand. Reading learners also like to read the information to clarify and consolidate after each session. Referring to publications where further information and key words are explained in more detail will aid learning.

Kinaesthetic Learners

Kinaesthetic preference students make up around 10 - 30% of the population. These students learn well through touch, movement and space, and learn skills by imitation and practice. They can appear slow if information is not presented in a style that suits them. During sessions they will like to have a go, touch, feel and experience the skill.

So, by adapting your teaching style to suit these groups, you should be able to create a learning environment with something for everyone.

Learning Styles

Once we have absorbed information, we need to process it in order for us to learn. In the same way that we have a preference for absorbing information, we also tend to have a preference for how we learn from this information. The same as people have a tendency towards left or right handedness which influences how they tackle manual tasks, many people have a particular learning style which influences how they approach mental tasks.

As instructor or coach, by being aware of the different learning styles we are able to modify our own style to suit that of our students.

Examples of Learning Styles

The following learning styles are stereotypes which most people fall into. There is no clear dividing line, as many people may conform to more than one style, depending on what they are doing.

Active Learners – *'I'll try anything once'*

Are enthusiastic and involve themselves fully in new experiences. They tend to act first and consider the consequences later, and tackle problems by brain storming and trying things out. They become easily bored and will generally dislike activities which require them to take a passive role.

Reflective Learners – *'I'd like time to think about this'*

Like to ponder experiences and observe things from different perspectives before reaching conclusions. They listen to others before making their own point and may like to stand back and observe and learn by listening and sharing ideas with others. They may prefer a slower pace and dislike taking action without having time to think.

Theoretical Learners – *'How does this fit?'*

Make sense of skills by understanding the theory behind them and think through problems logically, step-by-step. They like analysis and detail and may ask lots of questions. They learn best from activities which allow time to mix their observations with their theoretical knowledge, and enjoy having books, models and diagrams to study.

Pragmatists – *'How can I apply this in practice?'*

Think that if it works it's good. They are willing to try out new ideas to see if they work in practice and like to act quickly and confidently on ideas which attract them. Although they enjoy good demonstrations they become impatient with long winded explanations and discussions and learn best from practical sessions which allow them to test things for themselves.

"This excerpt has been taken from the Honey and Mumford Learning Styles Questionnaire, ©Peter Honey Publications Ltd, 10 Linden Avenue, Maidenhead, Berkshire SL6 6HB. A full online version of this questionnaire is available from www.peterhoney.com"

Tips for reinforcing learning
- Always put new skills into context. Understanding is helped if you see the 'big picture'.
- The average student can deal with approximately three to four chunks of information. Don't overload them.
- People remember the beginning and end, but often miss the middle. Keep demonstrations and explanations short and structured.
- Use a range of methods to teach important skills in order to cater for your students' range of learning styles, explaining, showing a video, visualizing, reading, etc.
- Ensure new skills become established with practice and reinforcement.
- Focus your students on what they should do, rather than what they shouldn't!

The Stages of Learning – From Unconscious Incompetence to Unconscious Competence
You can expect your students to largely follow the same cycle when learning new skills.

Unconscious Incompetence
Students don't know
what they don't know

Conscious Incompetence
Students are aware of what they don't
know. For some this adds clarity, others
find it daunting and frustrating

Unconscious Competence
Students are becoming competent but
still have to think about what they are
doing and how they do it. Following simple
sequences will be useful at this stage.

Unconscious Competence
Students now do things with very
little conscious thought.
Things flow and are effortless

Methods, Motivators and Barriers to Learning
Adults and young people often learn in different ways and for different reasons:

The way adults learn	The way young people learn
Typically more independent and self directed	More random and instructor/coach led
Goal orientated and structured approach to learning	Fun and experiential orientated approach
Need to know why they are learning something	Want to know 'what', 'where', 'when' and 'why'. Usually need to do things for a reason. Make it a fun exercise or game rather than just practice
Accumulated life experience can be applied to the learning process for good and bad	May be experiencing the skill for the first time. Not biased by other experiences – free learners!
Often reluctant to get things wrong, become frustrated when they do!	A more natural approach with fewer inhibitions. Happy to get things wrong!
Remember everyone enjoys learning if it's fun. Make your sessions fun and stimulating for all.	

What Might Motivate Students to Learn?

- Making or maintaining social relationships.
- Learning to engage others - parents often learn with a view to involving the rest of their family.
- A desire to achieve awards and qualifications.
- Escape or stimulation from everyday life.
- Interest in the subject.
- Lifestyle aspiration.
- Fear of failure.

Being aware of students' motivations for taking the course will help you to shape your course. This includes the materials you use and how you structure the groups in which they are placed for teaching.

Possible Barriers to Learning

- Other responsibilities (families, careers, social commitments).
- Lack of time.
- Environment – being wet and cold, or even too hot.
- Feelings – looking or feeling silly.
- Scheduling problems – when courses take place.
- Insufficient confidence.
- Inappropriate teaching methods.
- Personality clashes – between student and instructor.
- Being made to do course by parent or spouse, and not interested or ready to do it.

Fear

One of the main barriers a good instructor can help students overcome.

Adults and children normally have three principal fears when trying something for the first time:

1   Fear of failure

Be clear about students' progress throughout the course. Encourage them to try things out, even if it means making mistakes. If the course is being assessed, let students know the outcome.

2   Fear of the unknown

Keep students fully informed throughout the course, the stages and the reasons for the structure of the course.

3   Fear of not being liked or fitting in

Break the ice early and encourage groups to work together and get to know each other. Consider some games to help people relax.

PEOPLE SKILLS FOR INSTRUCTORS

What your Students Think of You

How you are perceived by others determines your credibility and therefore the influence you will have over them. First impressions are vital as it is estimated that up to 90% of people's opinions of you are formed in the first 10 seconds of meeting you. Therefore, you will start with a disadvantage if your students arrive for the course only to find you stressed and bedraggled, still trying to open up the centre, tidy up the mess, opening equipment stores and getting rescue boats afloat.

Tips for gaining your students' trust
- Always set up early and be ready for their arrival.
- Pay attention to your personal appearance – remember the all important first impression.
- Listen to your students and respect what they tell you. The more you listen, the more you can influence them.
- Spend time with them enabling a rapport to develop.

What you Need to Know about your Students

Remember that your students are going to have differing ages, genders, backgrounds, skills, hopes, fears, expectations and aspirations. It's a good idea to gather as much information as possible on these areas from your students prior to the course. Some of this can be done on the booking form or a simple questionnaire.

Questions you might want to ask beginners:
- Why do you want to learn to windsurf?
- Have you done any windsurfing before, when, where etc?
- Do you take part in any other water sports?
- What will you do when you are able to windsurf?

Being prepared with this information can help you to:
- Create the right environment.
- Be warm, welcoming and friendly.
- Tell them a bit about yourself.
- Get them talking about themselves.
- Tell them what to expect (and what not to expect).
- Create the course (together).
- Break the ice making them feel relaxed and part of the group.

Bribe Your Students!

Success as an instructor depends mainly on how well you can get on with a range of students of different ages, backgrounds and ability levels. Try creating the right conditions for them to learn using the **BRIBE** technique:

Begin
Repeat
Involve
Be creative
End

Begin

- Make everyone welcome.
- Introduce yourself.
- Check their expectations.
- Learn their goals and state your goals or give an overview.
- Engage the group with a good starting activity.

Repeat

- Help everyone absorb information by repeating skills in different ways to incorporate the styles on page 40.
- Use the metaphor: "It's rather like...." to reinforce new ideas.
- Summarise key points in each session and get your students to do this back to you.

Involve them with

- Tasks and activities.
- Questions – listening to the answers.
- Backtracking – using the exact words given by a member of the group.
- Checking group goals and the relevance/appropriateness to the group.
- Testing their understanding.

Be Creative

- Use lots of visual aids.
- Do the unusual and unexpected, with purpose.
- Tell stories, give real life examples and case histories.
- Get the audience to imagine what it would feel like if ....

End

- Summarise key messages.
- Give a metaphor – what it means.

COMMUNICATION SKILLS

Communication is more than just words. We are constantly communicating, even when we are not speaking.

Research has shown that
55% of communication is determined by body language, posture and eye contact.
38% by tone of voice, and only 7% by spoken words.
To get your message across, concentrate on how you speak, not just on what you say.
Typically students will:

- Filter – pick out the more or less important bits for themselves.
- Distort – interpret things for themselves.
- Delete – remove any bits that they find unclear or too difficult.

Remember that **Less is More**, keep your messages simple and free of jargon, and back them up with demonstrations and practical examples.

Check students' understanding of new information as often as possible, using open questions enabling them to confirm what you have said or what you want them to do.

Remember the worst question in the world is…"Do you understand?"

Non-verbal Messages
People use a variety of behaviour to maintain a smooth flow of communication, for example head-nods, smiles, frowns, laughter. Students' facial expressions will provide you with feedback on the session. Glazed or down-turned eyes indicate boredom or disinterest, as does fidgeting. Fully raised eyebrows signal disbelief and half raised indicate puzzlement. The posture of members of the group enables you to judge their attitude and mood.

Communication Blocks
Communication difficulties between instructor and student happen for a number of reasons:
- The student's perception of something is not the same as yours.
- The student may jump to a conclusion instead of working through the process of hearing, understanding and accepting.
- The student may lack the knowledge and understanding of what you are trying to teach.
- The student may lack motivation.
- The instructor may have difficulty in expressing what they want to say.
- Emotions may interfere in the communication process.
- There may be a clash of personalities.

METHODS OF INSTRUCTING AND COACHING   SECTION 5

Effective Communication

Contains six elements:

- **Clear**   Ensure that information is presented clearly.
- **Concise**   Do not lose the message by being long winded.
- **Correct**   Be accurate and avoid giving misleading information.
- **Complete**   Give all the information, not just part of it.
- **Courteous**   Be polite and non-threatening, avoid conflict.
- **Constructive**   Be positive, avoid being critical and negative.

Always check:

- You have your students' attention.
- Students are accepting what you are saying.
- You give clear explanations and demonstrations.
- Students have understood.

Always consider:

- **Why** you need to communicate.
- **Who** you are communicating with.
- **Where** and **when** the message will best be delivered.
- **What** you are explaining or demonstrating.
- **How** you get the information across.

Communication whilst afloat is particularly important but often goes wrong, so remember:

- Keep verbal communication to a minimum.
- Project your voice towards your students – it gets lost in the wind.
- Never shout.
- Position students where they can hear you best.
- Call students to you frequently for feedback and further instructions.
- Use pre-agreed visual signals.
- Use a thumbs-up signal to confirm understanding.

Be Positive

Whether ashore or afloat, always look for something positive to say first (however awful the attempt at a skill has been) and then provide information that will allow the student to improve their skills.

RYA Windsurfing Instructor Manual   47

PRESENTATION SKILLS

It is normal for an inexperienced instructor to be nervous about giving presentation despite the fact that they know their subject matter well. With the right frame of mind and a bit of practice, nerves will soon start to disappear. Being aware of these fears can help you to ensure that they don't come true.

Fear often revolves around things going wrong, such as:
- I'll dry up.
- No one will be interested.
- I'll be boring.
- They won't like me.
- I don't know enough about my subject.
- They'll ask me difficult questions.
- I'll make a fool of myself.

Good presentations depend on three elements:

The Words
- Clear, concise, jargon-free language.
- Think before you speak – don't think out loud!
- Emphasise the important bits.
- Summarise what you've said and ask questions.

The Music
- Vary your voice tone and pitch.
- Vary the pace.
- Speak in a conversational way.
- If you speak quickly build in pauses.
- Project your voice.
- Use silences, pausing before important points.
- Don't fade at the end of sentences.

The Dance
- Good posture, stand tall with shoulders down and back.
- Keep your head up.
- Make eye contact with all of the group.
- Standing or sitting? Decide which is best for you.
- Avoid distracting mannerisms, get a friend to tell you if you have any!
- Dress to help credibility. You can be smart and casual.

Before you Start your Presentation:

- Prepare yourself mentally.
- Look the group in the eyes establishing contact.
- Don't start speaking until you are fully in position and ready.
- Stop to breathe, look, listen, speak.
- An early smile helps to relax both you and your students.

Structuring presentations

The Beginning – Tell them what you are Going to Tell them

The opening few moments of a presentation are very important. You want the group to sit up and think 'this is going to be stimulating and important'.

Work out an introduction that will grab your group's attention. Tell them:
- What's in it for them.
- What you plan to cover and the structure (give headings).
- How long you will take.
- When they can ask questions.

If you are nervous, know your first few sentences off by heart and never apologise for your knowledge or speaking ability. Be relaxed and use a conversational tone.

Possible ways of opening are:
- Ask a question which requires a show of hands.
- Begin with a quotation or tell a story.
- Ask the audience to do something.
- Describe a true (and imaginary) situation.
- State a significant and challenging statistic.
- Challenge the audience.
- Tell a joke (but only if you are really good at this).

The Middle

After you've grabbed your group's attention with your introduction, move on to the main part of your presentation. Remember attention wanders and your students will pay most attention to the beginning and end of sections. Keep them short with clear headings and summaries. Be aware of (but not too self conscious of) your body movements:

Posture	Sit or stand up straight, but don't go rigid!
Hands	Don't be afraid of using them, as long as they are not a distraction.
Movement	Fine to move as long as it is around a distraction.
Position	Avoid obstructions to the audience's view of you.
View of your visual aids	Never turn your back on the group, they won't hear you.
Eyes	Maintain eye contact with the whole group.
Notes	Don't talk to your notes or visual aids.

The End – Tell them what you Told them

- Summarise your key points.
- Emphasise your themes.
- Make it significant.
- Do not end with something like 'that's about all I have to say so I'll end now'.
- Always stop before your audience want you to.
- Link back to your opening. For example, 'When I started, I said I would…'.
- Refer back to the original story or statistic.

Good Ways of Ending are:

- Issue a challenge.
- Appeal for action.
- Raise a laugh and tell a final anecdote.
- Point to the future.
- Finish with a quotation.
- Ask questions about what you've said.

Strategies for handling questions

Set the Rules for Questions

Set rules for questions in the beginning i.e. save questions for the end, or ask questions whenever you like (which might be more common and useful in an informal environment). Remember, you are the leader, so lead. Whichever rule you set, make sure it's followed. Reserve the right to stop taking questions in order to ensure you have sufficient time to cover all subjects.

What to Say when you don't know the Answer

Honesty is the only policy when presenting to a group, but blatantly admitting, "I don't know", in response to a direct question can be disastrous. No one can know the answer to every question, but it's how the situation is handled that separates great presenters from amateurs.

Don't get lulled into thinking you have seen and heard it all on a particular topic. Someone can come up with a question you have not thought of. The following strategies can help you field even the toughest questions with confidence.

1   **Reflection**

Repeat the question and pass it back to your group, "Does anyone here have any experience of that?" They can save you without realising it. They like to be involved and share their knowledge. After you have dealt with their contributions, summarise and add your own ideas.

2   **"I'll Get Back to You"**

This works well and is an opportunity, expand your knowledge, and impress your group. But remember to get back to them and don't just use it as an excuse!

3   **Defer to the Expert**

This is a more sophisticated version of the 'reflection' technique. Sometimes a question is legitimately outside of your area of expertise but there may be someone more experienced within the school or centre who you can pass it on to. You will need to decide who presents the answer – you or them.

Use of Visual Aids

Skilful use of visual aids can greatly enhance your presentation, but don't let them take over. Always remember that your relationship with your audience is key and visual aids are just there to support you.

Some General Tips

- The best visual aid is a live example of your subject matter i.e. the board and rig. Use them as often as you can.
- If the visual is too comprehensive, your audience will switch off from you and read the visual instead.
- Whenever possible use pictures, diagrams, graphs and colour rather than lots of writing.
- Do not use too many different visual aids as you can end up in a terrible muddle.
- Where possible, be interactive with your audience, making it more interesting and memorable.

Flip Charts work well for interaction
- Can be prepared in advance.
- Test your pens on the back of a sheet beforehand.
- Write a note for yourself in pencil (audience won't see).
- Blue tack up key sheets on the wall if appropriate.

Overhead transparencies are versatile and easy to prepare
- Ensure slides are in the right order (in a ring binder?).
- Limit the amount of information on each slide (4 lines, 4 words).
- Use colour (but red is very difficult to read).
- Switch off between slides (but not if it will become a distraction).
- Use your pen/pencil as a pointer.
- Use slides as notes.

Projectors are good for large, formal presentations.
- Ideal when photos are available.
- Probably need blackout.
- Use a pre-determined running order, so it's hard to improvise.
- May need an operator. If so, practise in advance.

PowerPoint is good for large, formal presentations
- Professional effect.
- Easy to update.
- Not as versatile as OHPs.
- Practise well beforehand.

Video can be inspiring if showing the professionals doing it really well
- Must be relevant and up to date.
- Use of video cameras for filming your students and playing footage of their own performance can be very powerful.

Whichever method you use, avoid:

- Too many words.
- Too much detail.
- Overcrowded slides.
- Bland images.
- Talking to the visual.
- Leaving the visual on display when you have finished with the subject matter.

Remember, consider your environment and ensure the visual aids you are using are suitable.

Making your Visual Aids Accessible

Every individual has a different perception of what they see and read. The shape and size of words can appear different to each reader. This is especially true when working with young people and students with dyslexia.

Consider that 10% of your clients may be dyslexic. Remember that changes you make to accommodate dyslexic people are good practice for everyone.

Adopting some simple strategies can help everyone to get the most from reading written information:

Font Style
- Fonts should be rounded with space between letters and reflecting ordinary writing. Fonts such as Arial or Comic Sans are good.
- Where possible use lower case letters rather than capitals. Using capital letters for emphasis can make text harder to read.

Paper
- Avoid light text on a dark background.
- Use coloured paper instead of white. Cream or off-white provides a good alternative.
- Matt paper is preferable to glossy paper, as this reduces glare.
- Ensure the paper is heavy enough to prevent text showing through from the back.

Presentation Style
- Limit lines to 60 to 70 characters to avoid putting strain on the eyes.
- Use short paragraphs with space between each line and paragraph.
- Use wide margins and headings.
- Use boxes for emphasising important text.
- Use bold to highlight words rather than italics or underlining.
- Keep lines left justified with a ragged right edge.
- Use bulleted or numbered lists.

Writing Style
- Write in short simple sentences.
- Be conscious of where sentences begin on the page. Starting a new sentence at the end of a line makes it harder to follow.
- Try to call the readers 'you'. Imagine they are sitting opposite you and you are talking to them directly.
- Give instructions clearly. Avoid long explanations.
- Stop and think before you start writing, so you are clear about what you want to say.
- Use short words where possible.
- Keep your sentences to an average of 15 to 20 words.
- Be concise.

Using Flipcharts
- Keep essential information grouped together.
- Print lower case rather than using joined writing.
- Flow charts or models are ideal for explaining procedures.
- Use pictures and diagrams.
- List 'do's' and 'don'ts' rather than continuous text.
- Use numbered lists rather than bulleted ones. Manually numbered lists work better with screen readers which may not read bullets aloud.
- Use small chunks of information, and plenty of white space, to improve readability.
- Use plain, simple and jargon-free language.
- Avoid red, orange or green as they can be hard to read for some people such as those with dyslexia.

BRIEFING AND DEBRIEFING

The instruction of windsurfing is essentially a practical process of brief - task - debrief. The students are there to use the equipment, enabling them do the tasks. The learning, assisted by tools such as simulators, really starts afloat and in particular when the student tries for themselves. The instructor's job is to make this experience enjoyable, informative and safe.

On a course you should get your students on the water as soon as possible. Students may be slightly anxious, however once people see a simple demonstration by the instructor and better still, try for themselves, they will pick up the concept fairly quickly. Providing the students with a straightforward and achievable task early on, followed by a genuine 'well done', will help them to relax and realise the course is achievable.

Briefings
Providing students with a clear brief avoids students having to remember a great deal of detailed information. Briefings can be divided into two parts:

General Briefings A briefing that is common to all activities afloat, such as "Everyone on the waterfront or afloat must wear a buoyancy aid". You may find that you need to remind people of briefings such as these now and again.

A general briefing could include:
- Clothing and buoyancy aid checks.
- Launching, landing and leaving your equipment safely ashore.
- Fire or emergency procedures.
- Any specific rigging and launching area.
- When to go on the water.
- Signals.

Remember – check if they understand, see the section below on 'Checking Understanding' for more information.

On the simulator, teaching is instant: 'put your feet here', 'move your hands to here'. But teaching and coaching becomes less predictable when you move on to the water. The prudent instructor will allow for this with an efficient briefing before the task and effective debrief after the task.

Without these, learning will only happen by accident, or if the student is able to analyse and modify their own performance.

Specific Briefing A briefing that should happen before every individual session, and the clue is in the title!

If it's too long, students will switch off, become disinterested and miss vital information that may affect their performance or safety.

The briefing should include areas such as:
- Aims and task of the session and how these are to be achieved. Don't duplicate the simulator session they've just had.
- Skills (demonstrated) to be practised.
- Timings.
- Windsurfing equipment and sails suitable for the exercise.
- Sailing area, including the boundaries, how they will be marked and any hazards to be aware of.
- Re-grouping area.
- What to do if the students go out of the area.
- Signals to be used (including general recall and abandon session).
- What the students should do in an emergency.

Checking Understanding

A briefing is only any good if the students understand it. Don't fall into the trap of checking their understanding by asking the classic question: 'Does everyone understand?' There will only ever be one answer: 'Yes'!

Instead, ask questions that relate to the information that's just been given, for example:
'Where are we going to sail?'
'What task are we going to perform?'
'What signal will I use to bring everyone back to the beach at the end?'

If the correct answers are coming back, it's likely that an effective brief has been given.

The classic telltale sign of a poor briefing is, when you move away to start the task, the students get into a huddle and ask each other 'What do we do?', 'What did the instructor say?'

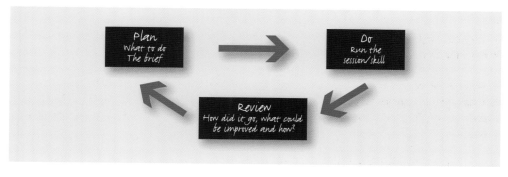

The task

The task must be chosen to suit the ability of the students. Part of the skill of instructing is to assess the student's ability and provide tuition at a challenging but not impossible level. It is very frustrating for someone with a natural flair or with some experience to be taught at the pace of the slowest beginner.

Once the task has been set, allow the student to feel responsible for it. Do not continually interrupt, if you have briefed well it should be unnecessary. Should a student misinterpret the task and things go wrong, a discreet chat will allow the student to correct the mistake while still being in control. Never dominate the task in order to demonstrate your skill, the idea is that they demonstrate theirs.

Occasionally, if appropriately carried out, allowing a mistake to be made can illustrate a point; this should only be done if you feel it is a good learning opportunity. Usually a technique more fitting to a higher level course, great care should be taken not to use the situation to put down or demoralise the student.

Do not hesitate to stop the session should other influences, such as a change in weather or students not making progress as expected, make your aims unachievable. Simply set a new task and re-brief the group.

Debriefing
Giving effective feedback is what separates the good instructors from the average ones. It is also a huge benefit to a student who would otherwise be learning from a book.

Delivering quality feedback isn't easy. For maximum impact, feedback should happen as soon after the task as possible. This implies that it should happen as, or just after, the student performs the skill. This may not always be possible for many reasons. If not, it should take place ashore once the group has returned, the kit has been made safe and the students are receptive. This may mean moving to a sheltered spot, having a drink and getting comfortable.

Your feedback needs to be more sophisticated than a collective 'Well done, that was great. How does everyone feel?' Each student needs information on what they achieved, what went well, what didn't go so well and how to improve.

There are two models commonly used for providing feedback, as follows:
The **hamburger** – It's tried and tested, but has been around for a long time now. Your students will eventually recognise the pattern.

The **traffic light** – It's along similar lines, but offers more opportunities for flowing discussion, which works well with most students.

You will sometimes have a student who just wants to be told what's going wrong and how they can put it right. If a student is happy with this approach, there's no harm in trying, so long as it's done with sensitivity.

For any method of feedback to work, some common elements need to be in place beforehand:
- Be clear with your students what the task is and how to perform it.
- Ensure that it is achievable by the students.
- Observe the session carefully.
- Record what happens. Take notes if necessary.
- Stay in charge of the session and safety throughout.

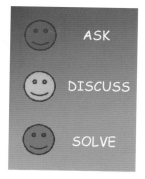

The hamburger

The traffic light

The **hamburger**

1   Build confidence by identifying positive/correct elements.
2   Consider what didn't go so well and how to correct it (around three points).
3   Suggest and agree on a positive action plan for improvement.

The **traffic light**

1   Ask the student about aspects of their performance. Start with open and general questions, and then focus on specific areas of performance.
2   Discuss these areas using the student's response to the questions.
3   Encourage the student to seek the solution. If they can't, do this for them. The student should always be the one who identifies the problem and then provides the solution, with guidance and help from the instructor.

By allowing the student to start analysing their performance and seeking ways of improving, they will learn how to continue this process well beyond the structured instructor-led session.

Providing Feedback as a Group or Individually

As discussed earlier, it is important that we create an environment for our students to receive their feedback effectively. Usually we find ourselves providing feedback to our students as a group, with each student learning from each others' mistakes or achievements.

However, individual feedback may be required in some situations, maybe when a 'shining star' is evident within the group and more difficult tasks may need to be set compared to the rest of the group, or a student with a behavioural problem having difficulty completing a task, therefore not quite achieving the level required to be issued with a certificate.

These examples and many more that you will experience while instructing should be dealt with individually and with care.

GROUP CONTROL

Having good group control creates an effective learning environment for both students and instructors. There are many influencing factors and, due to the teaching environment, some are easy to control while others are out of our immediate control.

What Factors Affect our Control?

Different factors will affect different centres depending on the location and courses they offer. Below are just a few of the main influences. The more experience an instructor gains, the more likely they will be able to pre-empt situations or deal with them as they occur. See if you can think of any more:

The Environment

Wind, tide and topography have an effect on how our sessions run. Strong or an increasing wind often creates a more complex environment for teaching, as can a sudden decrease, especially in a tidal environment.

Stronger winds mean things happen faster. For some sessions it can be a valuable ingredient, for others it can create challenging conditions that students will find tiring.

The Task

Some skills are much easier to control than others. Exercises for transitions such as tacking and gybing, can naturally keep a group close together. The addition of markers as visual parameters will also help.

When students are learning skills such as harness work and footstraps, they may require stronger winds to become more accomplished and therefore tend to need larger sailing areas which are naturally harder to control. As students are progressing in windsurfing they will naturally drift downwind, until they are proficient at tacking.

The Student(s)

Ensure the task set is achievable in the prevailing conditions. If students start to struggle, don't hesitate in stopping the exercise, re-grouping and setting a new achievable task. Having a designated place where students can rest increases the ability to keep the group together, reducing downwind drift and providing a place for feedback and/or further coaching.

Principles of Good Group Control

Gain an accurate forecast

We are reliant on the conditions around us, such as wind, tide and temperature. Gaining a forecast and outlook for the day of the course will ensure we can adjust our session accordingly. Although forecasting has advanced, it is still best to gain it on the actual day of the course, rather than too far in advance.

Prepare a Session Plan

A well organised and prepared session will go a long way to minimising unpredictable occurrences! For further information on writing a session plan see pages 73-75.

Choose your Sailing Area

Choosing a sailing area that is appropriate to the group's ability and the task ahead is crucial, but remember to discuss your plans with other instructors at the centre.

Should there be no choice in the sailing area, you may need to increase your students' challenges by adding buoys to sail around or within.

A good clear brief needs
- Clear aims.
- Demonstration.
- Sailing Area.
- Self Rescue – Teach your group to be self sufficient via the use of rescue techniques, the safety boat is not a taxi!
- Safety Signals (see below).
- Question to ensure understanding; timings, task etc.

Signals
- *Come to me* – Both hands on head (plus whistle).
- *You come to me* – One hand on head and point at an individual (plus whistle).
- *Go to a certain direction* – Whistle and point to direction.

Use of a Powerboat

Most tuition takes place board to board, but depending on the teaching environment you may need to teach from a powerboat. A powerboat can be an invaluable aid in stronger winds or tidal conditions, to maintain group control and effective coaching.

Designated Meeting Points

In addition to being an opportunity to pass on feedback/coaching points, choosing a meeting place to re-group, can provide a perfect opportunity to brief on the next activity, and will help keep the group together.

Communication

Good communication is key from the moment you greet your students, through to controlling the group during sessions afloat, and presenting the final debriefs at the end of the course. As you will have read in the 'Avoiding Complaints' section (pages 17-18), most complaints occur due to a lack of communication.

Top Tips
- Students' names – Try to learn names as early as possible, making the session personable and enabling specific attention to be gained.
- If covering large distances, ensure there are places to stop to regroup.
- Wait until the group has reconvened before briefing a new session or changing a current one.

Teaching the RYA Windsurfing Schemes

Introduction

The following chapter should be the most valuable in the delivery of the National and Youth Windsurfing Scheme. Split into a number of sections, the chapter covers an array of subjects with helpful advice and information.

Pages 62-63 **The National Windsurfing Coaching System – Fastfwd**

Page 64 **Assessing Ability**

A guide for assessing a student's ability on an RYA course written in conjunction with the appropriate logbook.

Pages 68-70 **Teaching the Youth Scheme**

Many instructors' first sessions will be with kids. This can be daunting in itself, but how do we encourage these first time participants to stick with the sport?

Pages 73-75 **Session Planning**

Planning and preparation is an essential to becoming an effective instructor. Understanding how to put together an effective, well timed, session plan with useful aims, objectives and exercises that break down individual skills, are just a few of the areas covered in this section.

Pages 76-126 **Session Aids**

Suggested session for teaching the skills in the National and Youth Windsurfing Syllabuses. The session plans should be used as a reference and guide, backed up by a combination of information gained during your instructor course, relevant RYA publications, online information and, most importantly, *a large dose of instructor's enthusiasm!*

Relevant Publications

National Windsurfing Scheme Logbooks:
- W1 – RYA Youth Windsurfing Scheme Syllabus & Logbook
- G47 – RYA National Windsurfing Scheme Syllabus & Logbook

Online information:
- Start Windsurfing Teaching Method (W4a)
- Intermediate Coaching Notes
- Advanced Coaching Notes

Handbooks
- G49 – RYA Start Windsurfing
- G51 – RYA Intermediate Windsurfing
- G52 – RYA Advanced Windsurfing

Additional RYA publications will also prove useful in increasing and improving our knowledge as instructors and the theory taught throughout the scheme.

The National Windsurfing Coaching System – Fastfwd

Technique expert, Simon Bornhoft, worked with RYA Windsurfing to provide the scheme with a simple coaching model. This model focuses on the exact skills and techniques required to really make a difference on the water.

In reality, 99% of people want to learn how to blast up and down and turn round. Effective coaching should address the end users' needs and focus on getting students quickly into the thrill of the sport. As any good instructor knows, a customer's success can be often down to one very small basic point that makes all the difference.

Fastfwd is an on-water coaching guide and self-reminder system which concentrates on cultivating skills that are an integral part of progression, and totally transferable into every area of the sport. It is embedded from the intermediate course of the scheme and upwards.

The Formula is simple, memorable and incredibly versatile, with five key elements that are supported by some very specific actions and techniques. While you might concentrate on one particular point at a time, the Formula works in a continuous circle and acts as a constant student and instructor prompt. So, starting with Vision, you'll regularly run through the Formula, until you home in on one particular element to sort out a problem, or emphasise a point. Perhaps later, if appropriate, you will choose to link the elements together.

The Formula is made up of 5 key elements that form the basis of our actions on a board…

Vision • Trim • (Counter) Balance • Power • Stance

You may already have your own interpretation of these terms and how each element can have its own particular merits, but here's an explanation of each element of the formula:

VISION *maintains our sailing line*
Where you look, your sailing line and how you use your head are always the first considerations before any other action. Try starting your coaching or diagnosis with Vision. Such a simple point, unquestionably the most important aspect of both coaching and improving technique.

TRIM *keeps the board flat*
A flat, stable platform increases the ease in which we can control the board and rig in any situation. All the actions we coach should refer back into Trim.

BALANCE *forms our framework*
OR 'Counter Balance' refers to our continuous objective of maintaining our distance from the rig (by extending the front arm) and always opposing and counter balancing the rig's pull, position and movement with our body.

POWER *channels the rig's forces*

Power refers to channelling the rig's forces, by sheeting the boom in, back and down. Critical in many skills learnt in windsurfing.

STANCE *is how we use our body*

Stance refers to how we position, angle and direct the rig's forces with our body. We can recommend some very specific actions to create a range of movement that maximises the effect of our body in a windsurfing environment.

Assessing Ability

The RYA windsurfing schemes provide an easy and accessible way to progress in windsurfing with certificated courses and ways to log progression. Publications W1 (Youth Windsurfing Scheme) and G47 (National Windsurfing Scheme) provide a comprehensive syllabus for both practical and theoretical content during an RYA course.

Youth Windsurfing Scheme
The syllabuses for each of the stages in the Training and Racing awards are clearly expressed in terms of competencies. As the student is able to do each item, it can be signed off. When all the items in a particular stage are completed, the certificate may be given. On any course, it is possible that some students will complete some extra items from the next stage, in which case those items can also be signed off – remember to use the *'try something different'* section in the logbook too!

National Windsurfing Scheme
The National Windsurfing Scheme exists to promote windsurfing in an enjoyable, safe and informative manner, providing people with the skills and confidence they need to pursue the sport. It is important that students enjoy their time afloat and improve their skills.
By the end of the course students should have achieved a practical understanding, but may still be making mistakes, typically using the correct techniques, but their manoeuvres will not always be successful; such a student may still be awarded a certificate.

The following information is a guide for assessing students' ability in conjunction with the appropriate logbook.

Throughout the Youth and National Scheme terms **'Knowledge of, Understand'** and **'Can'** are used to determine the level of competency required to successfully complete the course and gain a certificate.

Knowledge of the subject
The subject will be briefly explained. Familiarisation during the course, with information on where to find out more.

Understands the subject
The subject will be covered in greater depth. You will be asked to demonstrate a basic understanding and leave the course able to further develop your own skills in this area.

Can demonstrate a level of proficiency in the subject
Background theory and practical demonstrations will be covered in greater depth by the instructor, with repeated practice by the student until they can demonstrate good skills in the subject.

Youth Windsurfing Scheme

The RYA Youth Scheme has been designed to relate to the RYA National Windsurfing syllabus, providing ease of use and comparison, Youth Stage 2 is equivalent to Start Windsurfing, with Youth Stage 4 equivalent to Intermediate Windsurfing in the National Scheme.

The RYA racing scheme has three badges: Start, Intermediate and Advanced. Having completed Stage 1, students would be at the right level to give it a go.

Stage 1

All fun, no theory. During this course the children should get on the water and discover windsurfing. To be awarded the Stage 1 certificate, they will need to be able to sail to a chosen point on the water and return to where they started (in light winds).

Stage 2

Prior to taking part on a stage 2 course, children should hold the Stage 1 certificate or be of that ability. Still in light winds, sailors should be taught tacking and gybing, helping them sail towards and away from the wind, and on all points of sailing.

Stage 3

Prior to the course, a sailor should be of Stage 2 ability. With a mixture of theory and practical teaching, Fastfwd coaching is used to introduce beachstarting, harness technique and improve tacking and gybing in stronger winds. As a result, by the end of the course, students should be able to sail on all points of sailing in a variety of conditions, knowing when to tack and gybe, beachstart and use the harness to a basic standard.

Stage 4

This stage should build on a confident ability to tack, gybe and sail in the harness, introducing basic footstrap technique. On completion of Stage 4 they should be able to use the harness, know when to tack and gybe and show a basic ability to use the footstraps. Once completing Stage 4, a sailor should move onto the Advanced modules of the RYA National Scheme.

Start Racing

A prerequisite for this course is Youth Stage 1 and, on the completion of Start Racing, students should have built up a basic understanding of racing rules, courses, tactics, pre-race preparation and racing techniques.

Intermediate Racing

On gaining Start Racing, a student should be encouraged to gain one to two seasons racing experience at club/regional level, prior to being eligible to take the Intermediate racing course. On completion of this course a student would be equipped to comfortably compete at regional meets with a rounded understanding of pre, during and post-race knowledge.

Advanced Racing

Two seasons or more experience at regional/national racing is required prior to taking the Advanced Racing course. By the end of the course a high level of racing knowledge (rules, starting, tactics and strategy), pre-race preparation (equipment, health and fitness), mental preparation and techniques (starting, developing speed and pumping, turning, tactics and strategy) would be expected. It is suggested that a student on this course would be a regular attendee at squad coaching sessions.

Photo: Richard Langdon

National Windsurfing Scheme

The National scheme is about teaching our students skills that will help them throughout their windsurfing career. It is also the basis on which the personal sailing requirements are set for RYA Windsurfing Instructor qualifications (See pages 22-33 for further information).

Start Windsurfing

As the students need no previous experience, the Start Windsurfing course is designed to teach the basics of windsurfing, using the Start Windsurfing Teaching Method (W4a). After the course students should be able to sail to a chosen point on the water and return to where they started in light winds.

Intermediate Windsurfing

Prior to participating on an Intermediate Course it is important that students either hold the Start Windsurfing Certificate or are of that ability, using all points of sailing in light winds.

Non-planing

Students should learn new techniques, using the Fastfwd coaching model, and develop existing skills such as sailing on all points of sailing, but in stronger winds. Beachstarting and the non-planing carve gybe can be taught as separate clinics or as part of the course.

Planing

Through the use of the Fastfwd coaching formula, this course should develop the student's current skills and improve their stance and ability to get the board planing. The exhilaration of speed and their improved theory knowledge will develop to comfortable blasting in footstraps and harness, in planing conditions. As with intermediate non-planing, beachstarting and the non-planing carve gybe can be taught as separate clinics or as part of the course.

Advanced Windsurfing

Once completing the Intermediate course, Stage 4 of the Youth scheme or when comfortable in footstraps and harness in planing conditions, a student should be ready to move onto the Advanced course of the national scheme.

By the end of the course, students should have improved blasting control to aid early planing and be able to tack on a variety of boards in varying conditions. Additional clinics will help them master the waterstart, infamous planing gybe, advanced carving skills or the handling of bump and jump conditions.

Teaching the Youth Scheme

The RYA Youth Windsurfing Scheme combines training and racing into one logbook, providing a clear way to progress. It takes beginners from scratch, in bite size chunks, to hooking in and hanging on in no time. Each course builds on their skills and confidence along the way.

Students can record their achievements up to Stage 4, when they will have the skills and ability to progress to the Advanced course and clinics of the National Windsurfing Scheme.

Throughout Stages 1 to 4 there are 'take a challenge' elements. Not part of the main certificate, but just fun things for the group to try and get signed off.

Good Old-fashioned Fun!
Fun is fuelled by enthusiasm, which can be difficult when it's pouring with rain and freezing cold. However, fun is how kids will remember the course and skills covered. Getting wet with the group, being in with the latest craze, TV programme or film will bring all kinds of fun options to the sessions.

A group of eight year old girls will be very different to teach compared to a group of 14 year old boys, so ensure the session is pitched at the right level. Although they are following the same scheme, being adaptable is crucial.

The Taster Session
One of the best opportunities for converting children into windsurfers is the taster session. Every year thousands of children and adults get their first taste of a sport through a taster session. This is most commonly a two hour session organised by schools or groups such as the Scouts and Guides. It is important that instructors teaching the youth scheme have a basic understanding of how children learn and what equipment is suitable. In a two hour session you should aim to get a group of six starting off with board games and progressing on to the sailing position and turning around, with the aim of having fun while giving them the buzz.

> **REMEMBER - The RYA produces a free taster session certificate, so every child can go home showing what they have achieved and where they can do more.**

By getting the taster sessions right, the courses will fill themselves. Get them wrong and potential clients will be lost, potentially forever.

The youth scheme should be taught by using the same Start Windsurfing teaching method, but adaptations in the use of the method are required. The section 'Methods of Instructing and Coaching' (pages 35-60) discusses different approaches you may or may not be familiar with.

Equipment
One of the most important things to get right when teaching children is the equipment, and small equipment doesn't mean it's been designed for juniors. There is little point giving

children old 3.5m wave sails with a boom and a full size mast sticking out of the top. As with all sports, the wrong kit will give those that are learning a bad experience and perhaps even put them off for life.

Recent advances in equipment are making teaching so much more accessible. Negative experiences and watching children struggle to pull their sails up with the booms way overhead, pulling them off at the slightest puff of wind, should be a thing of the past.

As children progress through the scheme it is important to move towards tunable sails. Ask yourself *'would you dream of going out in planing conditions using a training sail with harness lines on?'* – Hopefully the answer is NO!

The budget restrictions that centres can have may restrict the amount of 'technical' rigs available. But it is important if you want to encourage young prodigies to stick with the sport. Most manufacturers today have an affordable and impressive range of boards and sails, covering everything from the first experience to chosen disciplines such as racing, freeride and freestyle.

If budgets are a problem, there is a range of options and adaptations enabling children to learn about the equipment and the wind in an enjoyable environment. If adult equipment is your only option, ensure it is adapted to teach children. Here are a few suggestions:

Rigging sticks – A rectangular piece of material and two sticks. Cheap and easy to make and incredibly effective for that initial experience or a strong wind alternative. They are easy to use, fun for all and a great way to introduce wind awareness and the basics of how a board works.

Setup – There is no point blowing the centre's budget on the right kit if it's not set up properly. Put a 1.5m rig on a large adult beginner's board and it's not going to turn around. Think basics – if the centre of effort can't reach behind the dagger board/centre of lateral resistance, it won't have directional stability. Match the right boards with the right rigs.

Children who are small enough to use a 2.5m rig don't need the volume of an adult beginner board (219L). Try to use something smaller such as a board the centre may be currently using for their intermediate adult courses (175L or 150L).

Unless designed specifically for kids most fins supplied with beginner/intermediate boards will create too much resistance, due to their length, in relation to a super-light children's rig.

Most introductory and progression boards are, or can be, supplied with plastic fins. If not, a few cheap second hand fins can be adapted and kept in reserve for your children's courses. Try cutting these cheap fins in half.

The correct equipment is just one of the essentials: Tuition should also be adapted, providing a safe, hands-on experience in a fun environment.

Safety Considerations

When working with juniors, always consider instructor responsibilities, child protection issues (see pages 10-15) and practical challenges such as the increased heat loss in children when compared to adults. Devoting time during staff training to develop activities on and off the water to support the youth scheme, may be crucial to successful youth participation at the centre.

Keeping them in the Sport

Through the Youth Scheme and initiatives such as T15 and Onboard (see pages 5-6), the RYA is continually working towards increasing initial experiences and ongoing participation. For further information on current RYA initiatives check out the RYA website.

Teaching Disabled Sailors

Teaching a disabled person to sail is exactly like teaching a non-disabled person. You mix common sense with experience and apply safe practice.

The overall objective is to learn how to sail effectively, develop confidence, enjoyment, a sense of achievement and to have fun. It is important to encourage maximum participation and activity. Do not prejudge a person's competence by their disability, but rather by their experience, knowledge and ability.

We are all individuals, each with different interests. Someone with a disability has ideas, makes plans, gets excited, even bloody minded. In short they are just like the rest of us. There is no need to adopt a different manner and vocabulary, or to feel sympathy or embarrassment. The important thing is to treat a disabled person as you would anyone else.

Communication is the Key to Success
It is essential that communication is a two way process. Key points to remember are:

- Never assume.
- Ask.
- Listen.
- Establish individual communication.
- Emphasise the ability not disability.
- Make the terminology/jargon clear.
- Build trust.
- Check understanding.
- Offer empathy not sympathy.
- Learn very basic sign language.

A disability is not a barrier to the successful completion of courses. All participants must be able to demonstrate their ability to complete the whole syllabus, but this can be achieved by proxy. It is worth bearing in mind that the candidate has to possess good communication and teaching skills as well as knowing how to undertake the manoeuvre.

Special Endorsements
The 'special endorsements' line of the Course Completion certificate should be treated with care. Do not list any disability unless it directly affects the holder's ability to handle the equipment, so the prosthesis that gives a user complete function is of no consequence. However, a visually impaired person may have the endorsement 'Requires visual assistance on the water'.

How RYA Sailability can Support your Training Needs
Attitudes to the inclusion of disabled people in sport are forever changing, but we know that the biggest barriers of all are the concerns of non-disabled people. The barriers are often born of ignorance and apprehension, but most significantly from a lack of awareness.

Without the numerous club members and RYA Sailability Volunteers there would be no support to organise so many sailing and windsurfing opportunities throughout the country. As groups expand and new ones start up, the demand for volunteers grows.

Disabled people want to go sailing and windsurfing, and often need a variety of support to enable them to do so. Some are totally independent; others may need help with transport, launching equipment etc. Volunteers do not have to be a sailor or paramedic to help someone get afloat. Every job is important, but it is essential to identify what job is best for them.

RYA Sailabllity offers two training packages that can support your group/club in both awareness and volunteer organisation.

RYA Sailability Awareness Training
A comprehensive training course that will allow and encourage helpers to become involved by alleviating their fear of disability, and give them the knowledge needed to enjoy their involvement to the full. The course covers the following areas:

- The needs of sailors with disabilities, both ashore and afloat.
- Improved communication skills.
- The use of current terminology to explain disability.
- The use of specialist equipment and adaptations.
- Moving, handling and transfer techniques.

At the end of the course all participants are given a booklet containing keynotes from the course and receive a course completion certificate, which can be pasted into the RYA National Windsurfing Scheme Syllabus & Logbook (G47).

To find out more information on RYA Sailability please contact 0844 556 9550, email: Sailability@rya.org.uk, or check out their website www.rya.org.uk/sailability

Practical Session Aids

Session Planning

Planning and preparation are essential in becoming an effective instructor. A good way to plan for a course or clinic is by creating a session plan. Once you have run a few similar courses or clinics planning will become quicker.

A session plan is a record produced by planning clear objectives and exercises. By identifying the objectives and the resources available, we can identify exercises and activities that will form the structure to a session.

Session plans can be used as a record of what needs to be, and has been covered. This record is useful when handing a group over to another instructor, or may be a requirement should a question be asked regarding the content of your course or clinic.

Most importantly, create a template that works for you. There a few examples below and further can be found on the RYA website. Remember to include the name of the course/clinic at the top of the page, including a date so that you can file and find it for future reference!

When planning your session, ensure you also think about the group's progression. During a week's course you will produce a number of different session plans. It is important to find out if there is a specific end goal, such as the group or an individual who is looking to gain a certificate, as this will dictate the content of your plans.

There are many ways to devise or lay out a session plan but the general content should be the same:

- Course type/name and date.
- Number in group.
- Session duration.
- Session aim and objectives.
- Group's current ability and level of knowledge.
- Group's age and gender.
- Medical conditions.
- Weather forecast (Tide, if applicable).
- Equipment – type and amount, including safety provision (powerboats/radios/mobiles etc).
- Sailing area – Any hazards or other water users.
- Facilities available/required.
- Exercises, including group dynamics (pairs, individual or whole); any recourses or external tools required (buoys, powerboats, whistle etc).
- Timing – Estimated time for each exercise, provides approximate overall timing.

Top Tips

- KISS – Keep it short and simple
- Test the sailors to see whether your session plan has translated into effective learning
- Time to learn – Make sure your session is manageable. Don't try to cram too much into a session as your students can only absorb a certain amount of information. Allow sufficient time in your session plan for your students to practice
- Learning styles – people learn in different ways, so remember it's essential to include different methods of putting something across. For further information on learning styles see pages 37-42
- Breaking down a skill into components will aid progression as it allows you to concentrate on a specific element as an example:

    Whole-part-whole (work on the whole skill, then a specific part, before bringing the whole skill back together)

    Part-part-whole (work on two specific but different parts of a skill and then bring it back together at the end of the exercise)

An example:
Part – Part – Whole
Intermediate Tacking

1 **Part** – Run an exercise concentrating on the specific foot work
2 **Part** – Run an exercise concentrating specifically on Vision going through the tack
3 **Whole** – Perform the whole skill combining the elements learnt by breaking the skill up and see if there has been an improvement.

EXAMPLE SESSION PLAN

Course/Clinic:	Date:	Time:	Number in Class:
Training Centre:		Length of Session:	

Aim:	
Equipment Required:	
Safety Cover:	
Radio/Mobile:	
Ability:	
Planned Learning Outcomes:	
Weather Forecast Outlook:	

Exercise	Teaching Points (To inc any specific learning outcomes)	Group Organisation (Individual, Pair, small or whole group)	Timing

Comments:

Action:

Start Windsurfing Teaching System

The RYA has developed a basic teaching method that introduces people to the sport in a quick and easy way. The content of this basic teaching system for Start Windsurfing is outlined below, clearly split into sections and described in session plans, for ease of use and understanding by both the instructor and student.

Each session plan should be backed up with the W4a Start Windsurfing Teaching Method (downloadable from the RYA website), G47 RYA National Windsurfing Scheme Syllabus & Logbook or, if teaching youths, W1 RYA Youth Windsurfing Scheme Syllabus & Logbook, G49 RYA Start Windsurfing and, most importantly, an instructor's enthusiasm and adaptations to the environment they are teaching in!

The method is split into two main sections – 'on shore' and 'on water' with theory time to be allocated during the course. The Onshore sections should be taught using a basic simulator, enabling the students to get to grips with new manoeuvres prior to heading out on to the water.

Designed to be broken down and taught in sections, the instructor should individually demonstrate sections II, III and IV of **On Shore 1** on the simulator. At the end of a session, each student should be given the opportunity to practise the section on the simulator and later on the water. This is an ideal opportunity for the instructor to provide the student with a little coaching and feedback in a controlled environment, prior to heading out onto the water.

Breaking down the teaching sequences further might aid students' learning, providing small sessions to concentrate on at a time. A suggestion might be: Sections of on shore 1 followed by sections of on water 1 practice, such as: Sections I and II, (this could also be broken down into smaller sections if necessary) followed by individual demonstrations and practice from Section III; Section IV; Section V. Further information on this is outlined within Session 8.

When students have a reasonable grasp of sailing across the wind, they should proceed to On Shore 2. The two sections of **On Shore 2** may be split, depending on conditions and the group's ability.

The Start Windsurfing Teaching Method

On Shore 1
   I   Introduction to Kit.
   II Getting Started.
       Secure Position.
       Static Turn.
       Sailing Position.
  (on water practice).
   III Steering the board.
   IV Tacking.
   V Safety.

On Water 1
Various short sessions encouraging students to achieve goals and learn progressively, incorporating instructor demonstrations and students sailing across the wind.

On Shore 2
Recap on shore 1.
Upwind and improved tacking.
Downwind and gybing.

On Water 2
Incorporating various sessions to introduce these elements progressively:
Upwind and improved tacking.
Downwind and gybing.

Theory – (to be taught as appropriate to teaching sequence).
Sail Safe, basic sailing theory and terms and appropriate rescue elements.

Evaluating your Students' Ability
To ensure the students can be awarded with a Start Windsurfing certificate, the instructor needs to have covered all areas of the syllabus outlined in G47 RYA National Windsurfing Scheme Syllabus & Logbook during the course. There are many ways to assess a student to see whether they understand or can perform each area of the syllabus. For example, a triangular course may be the easiest option to assess their ability to tack, gybe and sail on all points, but there are lots of alternatives. Get creative and have fun with the group.

Definitions used During the Teaching Method
Teaching points – the procedure the instructor follows, key teaching points may be underlined.
Teaching sequence – the order of delivery.
Coaching points – key, simplified points that help to make a skill achievable.

Model for RYA Windsurfing Instructor Simulator Demonstrations

As with all presentations, there is a common formula to be followed to construct a meaningful demonstration. This model has four distinct stages:

1 Introduction

Introduce the task, the reason for doing it and how it fits into the overall programme.

2 Demonstration

Instructor demonstrates using simple, uncomplicated language.

3 Student attempt

Each student attempts each manoeuvre, corrective feedback is provided by the instructor, who uses each student to emphasise important coaching points.

4 Summary

Off the simulator, the instructor provides a final summary of what has been achieved and how it fits in the overall programme.

Session 1

ON SHORE 1
I INTRODUCTION TO KIT

This first session should provide the students with a brief introduction to the equipment they will be using during their Start Windsurfing course.

During the instructor's rigging demonstration, as much hands-on experience as possible should be gained by the students. Rig assembly can be a complicated process involving a number of crucial sequences. With many groups, rigging may best be done in stages, with the instructor showing a small part, then the students copying with their rigs and returning to the instructor for the next stage.

The board and rig used for the demonstration must be identical to that used by the students. Avoid introducing technical jargon if possible, but do use the proper terms for each item.

Aim
To give a brief introduction to the course, outline the session plan, show the function of various components of the board and rig and, if appropriate, demonstrate rigging or basic tuning techniques.

Group Dynamics
Teaching Location: Sheltered, close to launch site.
Teaching aids: A student board with the rig (de-rigged or into whatever state the students will find their own).

Information to be Covered
The function of each component, but be careful not to introduce new terms unnecessarily. Demonstrate how the equipment is rigged and made ready to sail.

Teaching Sequence
The board
- The front, back, top and bottom.
- Fin and daggerboard/centreboard operation.
- Mastfoot fitting.
- Centreline.

The rig
- The mast, boom, sail, mastfoot and uphaul.
- Sail onto mast and attach mastfoot.
- Boom height.
- Tensioning of the sail (downhaul and outhaul).

Completion
- Wind awareness and how to pick up the rig and carry it.
- Connecting the board and sail together.
- Storing the rig.

Coaching Notes
You may wish students to rig their sails at this point or just before they go on the water. Depending on centre requirements, full or even partial rigging may not be an option. If this is the case, students should be taken through the steps of rigging at some point during the course.

Exercise and Games
It may be appropriate to set exercises in carrying rigs to establish wind awareness, and the safety of others.

Learner Support Material
W4a – Start Windsurfing Teaching Method
G47 – RYA National Windsurfing Scheme Syllabus & Logbook
W1 – RYA Youth Windsurfing Scheme Syllabus & Logbook
G49 – RYA Start Windsurfing

Session 2

II GETTING STARTED – SECURE POSITION

A combination of skills are taught to the students during the getting going section, enabling them to be able to sail across the wind. These are the secure position, turning the board and the sailing position. Each demo should be clear and help to build progressive links.

Aim
To teach the student how to climb onto the board, pull the rig out of the water, get into and maintain the board in the secure position.

Group Dynamics
Ideal teaching location – Clean wind and a soft surface.
Teaching aids – Beginners' simulator with board and rig.

Information to be Covered
It is important that when the students are on the simulator they understand why the board must be manoeuvred and held in the SECURE POSITION.
Demonstrate all stages and encourage candidates onto the simulator to ensure they understand the importance of key positions and actions. Coaching points are emphasised to the candidates at the same time.

Teaching Sequence
1   Approach the board from the opposite side to the rig.
2   Place *hands on the centreline of the board* (shoulder width apart, with the front hand near the mast foot) and pull body over board.
3   Place knees on the board, keeping *weight over the centreline*. Reach and grab uphaul for stability.
4   Check wind direction. You may need to demonstrate or explain upwind rig recovery afloat.
5   Position feet equally either side of the mast foot on the centreline of the board, about a shoulder width apart.
6   Hold the uphaul rope with *straight arms* and stand up. Lean back slightly.
7   Keeping the mast at 90° to the centreline of the board, bend the knees slightly and using legs not back, pull the rig partially clear of the water.
8   Work hand over hand up the uphaul to pull the rig right out of the water. *Grasp the mast below the boom* with both hands, keeping arms extended.
9   Lean *the rig towards the back of the board* and the front will turn towards the wind.
10 Lean the rig towards the front of the board and the front turns away from the wind.
11 With the rig flapping freely and the board at 90° to the rig, this is the SECURE POSITION.

Coaching Points – to be highlighted by the instructor during candidate simulator sessions and continued during on water sessions
- Keep weight over the centreline of the board.
- Maintain feet position.
- Use legs, not back, to pull rig out of water.
- Keep head up.
- Maintain a comfortable relaxed position, arms extended, knees slightly bent and head up, (a V shape will formed between body and rig).

Learner Support Material
W4a – Start Windsurfing Teaching Method
G47 – RYA National Windsurfing Scheme Syllabus & Logbook
W1 – RYA Youth Windsurfing Scheme Syllabus & Logbook
G49 – RYA Start Windsurfing

Session 3

STATIC TURN

Aim
To turn the board through 180° either towards or away from the wind as required and, once completed, returning to the SECURE POSITION.

Group Dynamics
Ideal teaching location – Clean wind and a soft surface.
Teaching aids – Beginners' simulator with board and rig.

Teaching Points
Demonstrate the steering once in each direction.
Students should be encouraged to give feedback as a means of checking understanding.

Teaching Sequence (from SECURE POSITION, turning the board towards the wind)
1   Lean the rig towards the back of the board.
2   As the front of the board turns towards the wind *take small steps* around the front of the mastfoot.
3   *Keep the rig inclined* and move the sail across the back of the board.
4   Resume new SECURE POSITION having turned the board through 180°.

Coaching Points
Take small steps when moving feet around the mastfoot.
The further you incline the rig towards the back of the board, the faster the board will turn.
Ensure that feet and body are correctly re-positioned in SECURE POSITION after each turn.

This demonstration can be altered and used to show a turn away from the wind if required. Some students will find a turn away from the wind easier at first. The instructor should be confident that their teaching environment is suitable and take into consideration downwind drift.

Learner Support Material
W4a – Start Windsurfing Teaching Method
G47 – RYA National Windsurfing Scheme Syllabus & Logbook
W1 – RYA Youth Windsurfing Scheme Syllabus & Logbook
G49 – RYA Start Windsurfing

Session 4

SAILING POSITION

Aim
To teach the student how to get into the SAILING POSITION.

Group Dynamics
Ideal teaching location – Clean wind and a soft surface.
Teaching aids – Beginners' simulator with board and rig.

Teaching Points
Two demonstrations are required: the first to show the actions and the second to show it as a flowing movement.

Teaching Sequence (from SECURE POSITION)
1   Select and look at a *goal point ahead,* checking for obstructions.
2   Take your front hand off the mast, moving it across your body and onto the boom.
3   Take your *back hand off* the mast.
4   Step back with your back foot <u>behind the daggerboard</u>, sliding your front foot back behind the mastfoot facing forwards.
5a Turn your shoulders towards your goal point, drawing the rig across your body and forwards by extending the front arm and taking the rig to the balance point.
5b (At the same time) Bend your back leg, drop your body weight back and place your back hand on the boom, pulling in the sail gently to create power.
6   Keep looking at your *goal point*, re-position feet, hands and body until comfortable.
7   To stop, let go with the back hand and return to the secure position.

Coaching Points (to be brought out in a second demo)
- Establish a goal point across the wind.
- Ensure that the rig is pulled to the balance point. Emphasise a smooth flowing movement throughout.
- The power generated by the rig has to be counter balanced by body weight.
- Power can be released by easing out with the back hand, and increased by pulling in. Increase body weight on the back foot as the power increases.

Learner Support Material
W4a – Start Windsurfing Teaching Method
G47 – RYA National Windsurfing Scheme Syllabus & Logbook
W1 – RYA Youth Windsurfing Scheme Syllabus & Logbook
G49 – RYA Start Windsurfing

Session 5

III STEERING THE BOARD

Aim
To teach students to steer the board towards and away from the wind.

Group Dynamics
Ideal teaching location – Clean wind and a soft surface.
Teaching aids – Beginners' simulator with board and rig.

Teaching Points
Demonstrate only once. It should be explained that the purpose of this section is to make small adjustments in course, as if to avoid an object in the water some distance ahead. Keep your explanations simple.

Teaching Sequence (from the Sailing position)
Towards the wind
1 Look upwind and choose a *new goal closer to the wind.*
2 Lean *the rig back,* extending the back arm. The front of the board will turn towards the wind.
3 When heading towards the new goal, *return the rig to the sailing position,* pulling in slightly with your back hand.

Away from the wind: (from new sailing position)
4 Keeping the body low, *lean the rig forwards and slightly towards the wind,* extending the front arm. The front of the board will turn away from the wind.
5 When heading towards the original goal point, *return the rig to the sailing position* and ease out slightly with the back hand.
6 The board should now be sailing to the original goal point.

Coaching Points
* Looking at your goal point.
* Awareness of wind direction.
* Counter balance the rig with the body.

Learner Support Material
W4a – Start Windsurfing Teaching Method
G47 – RYA National Windsurfing Scheme Syllabus & Logbook
W1 – RYA Youth Windsurfing Scheme Syllabus & Logbook
G49 – RYA Start Windsurfing

Session 6

IV TACKING

Aim
To improve tacking while making the turn more effective and stable.

Group Dynamics
Ideal teaching location – Clean wind and a soft surface.
Teaching aids – Beginners' simulator with board and rig.

Teaching Points
The students already know the principles of a static turn. These skills can now be refined and improved. Demonstrate the turn twice, once in each direction.

Teaching Sequence (from sailing across the wind)
1   Choose and steer towards a goal point closer to the wind.
2   Return the rig to the correct sailing position, pulling in slightly with your back hand.
3   Check for obstructions.
4   Move the front hand to the mast and *front foot in front of the mast.*
5   Steer the *board towards the wind* by leaning *the rig leant back* and extending the back arm.
6   As the board turns into the wind, *step up with both feet in front of mast, transferring the back hand* to the mast at the same time.
7   Keep the rig inclined and move it over the back of the board until the turn is completed.

Resume the SAILING POSITION on the opposite direction and move off.

Coaching Points
- Wind awareness.
- Keeping the rig moving across the back of the board.

Exercise and Games
Specific tasks/goals will help the student to achieve the desired skills. See the exercises in On Water 1 (page 89) for appropriate examples.

Learner Support Material
W4a – Start Windsurfing Teaching Method
G47 – RYA National Windsurfing Scheme Syllabus & Logbook
W1 – RYA Youth Windsurfing Scheme Syllabus & Logbook
G49 – RYA Start Windsurfing

Session 7

V SAFETY

Aim
To make students aware of safety issues and various methods of self-rescue.

Group Dynamics
The methods can be demonstrated on the simulator or on the water, by the instructor. Candidates can practise on the water (if appropriate).

Teaching Points
Instructors should describe the situation in which self-rescue should be considered, and the alternatives available.

Method 1 – Butterfly Method
Instructors must be aware of the restrictions due to the development of shorter wide style boards, and teach as appropriate. In no wind or light wind, an inability to sail can be easily and quickly remedied with the butterfly method.

Advantages
Very quick and efficient.
Good for short distances in little or no wind.

Disadvantages
Difficult to:
Maintain the sail's balance in choppy conditions.
Perform in medium to strong wind conditions.
Perform on shorter wide style beginners boards.

Method 2 – Flagging

An inability to sail downwind can be
remedied by flagging downwind.
This can also be an effective first
introduction to guiding students to
sail and steer the board downwind.

Advantages

Possible in any wind strength.
Quick and easy.

Disadvantages

Not easy to balance in chop.

Method 3 – Full De-rig Self Rescue

This method may be required to
self-rescue, be towed or rescued by
a boat. Use of the full de-rig to self-
rescue should be considered as a
last resort as re-rigging in open water
is extremely difficult.

This method at principal's discretion
and is not an essential part of the
candidates' course.

It is recommended that students
should sail at an RYA centre or
where safety cover is provided.
The student should also be given
information about progressing on
to the RYA intermediate course.

Session 8

ON WATER ONE

Aim
During this session, students should be issued with the relevant clothing, told how to wear it and have the importance of doing up buoyancy aids and wetsuits fully explained before heading out on to the water. The On Water one session should comprise short sessions mixed with the simulator demonstrations and student practice.

Group Dynamics
On Water One should comprise a number of short sessions which encourage the students to achieve goals and learn progressively. Make sure students' goals are visible, such as the use of marker buoys.

Teaching Location
There should be a site specific safety brief, with the instructor encouraging safety awareness and an attitude of self responsibility among the students. The briefing MUST include the limits of the sailing area and the signals for recall to the shore.

Coaching Points
Balance exercises can be used to begin the first on-water session. There are many purposes to these exercises:
- 'Break the ice' between a group of students.
- Develop confidence in the water with a board.
- Familiarise themselves with the stability of the board.
- Discover how the daggerboard/centreboard works.

Instructor Demonstration
The instructor should demonstrate sections II to IV of On Shore one on the water. Section V (safety) can be talked about before going afloat or during a break in the Sailing lesson 1.

Sailing Practice
A period of sailing across the wind making use of all sections of On Shore one (with the instructor in close attendance) will follow. When the students are reasonably competent the instructor can continue with On Shore two.

Powered Craft
Instructors needing to teach from a powered craft should remember that it is a coaching tool to be used conservatively when in close proximity to the students. When towing or returning a student from downwind, take the opportunity to give the student constructive feedback and fault analysis.

Exercise Suggestions

Exercise 1 Aim   Balance exercises (centre option).

Exercise 2 Aim   Static turning exercises – Either up/downwind or both.

Exercise 3 Aim   Sailing position – Sailing across the wind using the static turn.

Exercise 4 Aim   Sail across the wind – Holding ground using the tack.

Exercise 5 Aim   Sail across the wind – Steering.
Emphasis on steering – Basic steering towards and away from the wind.
A figure of 8 course may be useful for students.

Exercise 6 Aim   Appropriate theory.

Coaching Points

Once students are on the water they will progress at differing rates. The instructor should take care to spread time fairly between all students. Varying abilities in the group may make the decision about when to bring students off the water for On Shore two difficult.
After a break students should be ready and able to progress on to the next stage or further practice.

When the students are reasonably competent the instructor continues with On Shore two.

Session 9

ON SHORE TWO – UPWIND AND IMPROVED TACKING

Aim
To introduce progressive sailing upwind and how this can be achieved by sailing closer to the wind and improving the tacks learnt in On Shore one. Students need to be given a clear example of the concepts of wind awareness and the No Go Zone prior to upwind simulator or on water demonstration.

Group Dynamics
Ideal teaching location – clear wind and a soft surface.
Teaching aids – beginners' simulator with board and rig.

Information to be Covered
It is a good idea to recap On Shore one (getting started, steering and tacking) especially if there has been a significant break. The students already know the principles of altering course and tacking. These skills now need refining, focusing on sailing closer to the wind and holding course.

Demonstrate sailing upwind with clear progression and tacking twice, once in each direction. Identify a goal directly upwind and explain how progress can be made. Improved tacking and holding course on an upwind goal/sailing line with relation to the no go zone.

Teaching Sequence (from the Sailing Position)
1   Identify a new goal closer to the wind.
2   Look at the upwind goal and steer the board towards the new goal (as learnt in On Water one).
3   Hold this course – the board is now sailing and making progress closer to the wind, in the correct sailing position.
4   To tack, check for obstructions.
5   Tack the board (as per On Water one). Resume sailing position in the opposite direction and move off.
6   Demonstrate in a variety of directions, showing progression (and zig-zagging) upwind, repeating if necessary to provide the students with sufficient examples.

Coaching Points

- Making clear progress upwind. No Go Zone.
- Wind awareness.
- Smooth and flowing movement.
- Keep sail pulled in when close hauled.
- See exercises written under On Water two (page 95).

Learner Support Material

W4a – Start Windsurfing Teaching Method
G47 – RYA National Windsurfing Scheme Syllabus & Logbook
W1 – RYA Youth Windsurfing Scheme Syllabus & Logbook
G49 – RYA Start Windsurfing

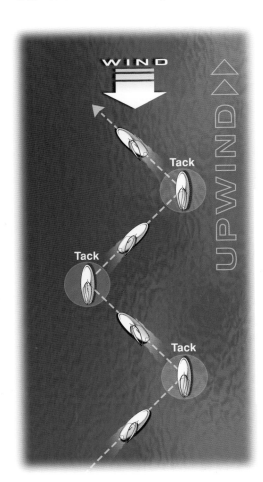

HOT TOP TIP

Flagging

Having sailed upwind a useful way of getting back downwind is to practise the self-rescue technique of flagging.

Session 10

DOWNWIND AND GYBING - SECTION A

Aim
To introduce the concepts of downwind sailing and gybing.

Group Dynamics
Ideal teaching location – clean wind and a soft surface.
Teaching aids – beginners' simulator with board and rig.

Teaching Points
ONLY the instructor demonstrates this section on the simulator. Students <u>must</u> practise on the water.

Information to be Covered
This section of On Shore two contains separate concepts;
Steering away from the wind, sailing on a broad reach and gybing,
Running and steering on a run.

Teaching Sequence (from a Sailing Position Across the Wind)
Sequence A – Steering away from the wind, sailing on a broad reach and gybing

1   Steer the board away from the wind (as in On Water one and recapped below).
2   Keeping the body low, continue to steer away from the wind by leaning the rig forward and slightly towards the wind, extending the front arm. The front of the board will turn away from the wind.
3   Hold this position until the board is on a run.
4   To gybe, ease the sail out with the back hand.
5   Foot change – Move your front foot back, just in front of the back foot, and your back foot forward towards the mast, keeping weight over the centreline.
6   Rig change – Slide your front hand towards the mast, let go with the backhand and transfer it across your body and onto the new boom, releasing the front hand.
7   Look at the new goal point across the wind and resume your sailing position.

Coaching Points
- Instructor demonstrates a second time to reinforce.
- Further coaching is done on the water, as there is no student practice on the simulator.

Learner Support Material
W4a – Start Windsurfing Teaching Method
G47 – RYA National Windsurfing Scheme Syllabus & Logbook
W1 – RYA Youth Windsurfing Scheme Syllabus & Logbook
G49 – RYA Start Windsurfing

Session 11

SAILING ON A RUN - SECTION B

TO BE INCLUDED AT CENTRE REQUIREMENT

Aim
A centre may want instructors to introduce the students to running and steering downwind. Students may find it easier to run and steer on a run once they have experimented with 'flagging' downwind with no power in the rig.

Group Dynamics
Ideal teaching location – clean wind and a soft surface.
Teaching aids – beginners' simulator with board and rig.

Teaching Points
ONLY the instructor demonstrates this section on the simulator, students must practise on the water.

Teaching Sequence – (Section B: running and steering on a run, from the sailing position)

1   Steer the board away from the wind, holding this position until the board is pointing downwind and on a run.
2   Ease the sail out with the backhand. At the same time, move the front foot back, keeping both feet either side of the centreline.
3   The sail is now across (at 90°) the centreline of the board. This is running.
4   By transferring bodyweight and/or leaning the rig to the left, the front of the board will turn right.
5   By transferring body weight and/or leaning the rig to the right, the front of the board will turn to the left.
6   If body weight and rig are kept over the centreline of the board, it will continue in a straight line.
7   In stronger winds, move body weight further back on the board and bend the knees to maintain balance and control.
8   To change direction; gybe and resume the sailing position.

Learner Support Material
W4a – Start Windsurfing Teaching Method
G47 – RYA National Windsurfing Scheme Syllabus & Logbook
W1 – RYA Youth Windsurfing Scheme Syllabus & Logbook
G49 – RYA Start Windsurfing

Session 12

ON WATER TWO

Aim
Instructor should be encouraged to take to the water to demonstrate On Water two, and then provide coaching to individuals as they try a series of upwind and downwind exercises. Once students have been taught downwind sailing, they will find a new freedom to travel distances on all points of sailing.

Group Dynamics
Setting good limits to the sailing area will help group control. The limits can be productively achieved by setting a course or point to aim for. Your students need to use their newly learnt skills to achieve the ultimate goal of the Start Windsurfing course, to be able to 'make progress upwind and downwind using tacking and gybing in light winds. This could be managed by setting a journey or triangular course, depending on the location.

Exercise and Games
Numerous tasks will help students to achieve the desired skills. Upwind buoys as goals are particularly useful, provided realistic distances are set.

Exercise 1 Aim	Sailing across the wind. Recap if required.
Exercise 2 Aim	Upwind and tacking combo.
Exercise 3 Aim	Steering and power control towards or away from the wind.
	Practising holding course and making steps towards and away from the wind.

As an example, a student is struggling with power in the rig when steering downwind. To achieve a gybe do progressively deeper steers downwind without actually doing a gybe. This helps students build confidence and the instructor can increase the amount steered each time until students go through the downwind position and complete a gybe.

Exercise 4 Aim	Zig-zagging downwind and gybing combo.
Exercise 5 Aim	Downwind and introducing a run (location specific).
	Steering downwind and gybing exercises.
Exercise 6 Aim	Follow my leader – Particularly appropriate for developing and refining upwind work.

Students should now be armed with the skills to maintain their position, sail across the wind and make way towards an upwind goal and return sailing downwind.

Theory
The theory outlined in the Start Windsurfing syllabus should be covered as the course progresses. Every opportunity should be taken at this stage to recap on the principles of sailing and more essentially on safety aspects.

Towards the end, or on completion, of the Start Windsurfing course the instructor should make the students aware of what steps they can take next and the opportunities available to them, including club activities and the next course – Intermediate Windsurfing.

Intermediate Windsurfing Teaching System

The following pages will help you set out sessions, covering specific skills from the intermediate syllabus and coaching model, improving on the basic skills your students have learn during their Start Windsurfing Course.

Students looking to move on to the Intermediate section of the national scheme should either hold the Start Windsurfing certificate or fulfil the sailing ability as outlined in G47 RYA National Windsurfing Scheme Syllabus & Logbook.

Intermediate is the first level where the coaching model Fastfwd is introduced, aiding a smooth progression from the skills learnt during their Start Windsurfing Course. To ensure this is a seamless advance, it will be a good idea to introduce the formula as one of the first sessions you run. Further information of the coaching model is on pages 62-63.

For many of your students this is an exciting stage of their windsurfing career, so let's make it a fun and enjoyable experience. One of the key elements enabling us to do this is the equipment we provide during the course and how we introduce it. Initially, students may find this transition a little daunting, and a few may feel they have stepped back rather than progressed, a minor, but important hurdle for you to provide specific coaching tips, especially with the exhilaration they are about to experience!

The intermediate course and clinics should be taught on modern boards and rigs. Boards should initially be of a volume around 190 to 170 litres, fitted with footstraps and in early stages continue to have a daggerboard. Progressing onto a fully battened rig, fitted with harness lines, is also essential at this stage of our student's development.

Standard course
Introducing the Formula
    Vision
    Trim
    Balance
    Power
    Stance

Preparing to Launch

Getting Going

Harness

Footstraps

Blasting Control

Steering

Tacking

Standard Clinics
Beachstarts

The Non-Planing Carve Gybe

Session 1

INTRODUCTION TO THE FORMULA

Aim

To familiarise the group with the Formula terminology by practical demonstration, showing how the elements of the Formula fit together. To give a clear and structured introduction to the values and concept of the Fastfwd Formula, providing a brief outline of the key elements.

To provide the students with simple, concise guidance for each of the elements. You can always recap back at a later stage. This will enable you to be more simplistic, less wordy and very effective in your coaching.

Objectives

By the end of the session students should:
- have an understanding of the Fastfwd coaching formula.
- have a basic understanding of the key elements.
- understand how the Formula fits into other areas of their sailing.

Group Dynamics

This session is based around a simulator, with the instructor demonstrating the Formula. Remember, the longer the session takes, the longer it will be before you get onto the water.

Learner Support Material

G51 – RYA Intermediate Windsurfing
Intermediate Coaching Notes (www.rya.org.uk)

Session 2

PREPARE TO LAUNCH

Aim
Introduce the concept of correct equipment set up for the students' boards and rigs. It is important that students are aware of how important it is to have their equipment tuned correctly to suit them and the conditions. Try out your students' equipment to check it is rigged correctly whenever possible.

Safe launching and landing skills and procedures should also be covered during this session.

Objectives
By the end of the session students should:
- Have some basic knowledge of board and rig tuning.
- Have an awareness of launching and landing skills.

Group Dynamics
This is a land-based session, preparing the candidates to go afloat. Information to be covered:
- Correct rigging technique.
- Board tuning.
    Fin placement, size according to sail size and conditions.
    Footstraps placement and adjustment.
    Mast base placement.
    Boom set up and height.
    Harness Line positioning, width and length.
    Harness type and fit.
    Sail tuning.
    Daggerboard.

- Launching and landing.
    Check, check, check.

Coaching Notes
This session can be extended or shortened to suit weather conditions. Depending on conditions, operating area and the group's experience you may decide to run a beachstart session (see page 107) before going afloat.

Be aware that some of your students may not be confident at launching and landing in windy conditions, or in groups of people. It is important that all safety angles are covered. All candidates should be in suitable clothing with harnesses, and/or buoyancy aids.

Learner Support Material
G51 – RYA Intermediate Windsurfing
Intermediate Coaching Notes (www.rya.org.uk)

Session 3

GETTING GOING

Aim
To encourage students to use the Formula to get the board going earlier in both light and strong winds. Introduce a 'drop and push' to help acceleration and use a simulator to show students how the Formula is used to create a more efficient and dynamic body position to encourage early planing in light and strong winds.

Objectives
By the end of this session the student should be able to adopt different body positions in order to get the board going, or even planing earlier.

Group Dynamics
This is a relatively short session (depending on conditions) with an instructor demo on the simulator, followed by instructor demo on the water and a water based session with student practice and instructor feedback.

Information to be Covered
- Drop and push.
- Drop and dig.
- Stances: Straight 7 'Lift and lock', Super 7.

Exercises or Follow-up Work
- Experimenting with sailing line, feet and body positions.

Learner Support Material
G51 – RYA Intermediate Windsurfing
Intermediate Coaching Notes (www.rya.org.uk)

Coaches' Corner – Key terms in Getting Going:

DROP AND DIG
A dynamic stance. THE DROP – The body led by the hips moves down and out, pushing and resisting against the windward rail with equally weighted feet. THE DIG – Drive through the heels.

DROP AND PUSH
A dynamic stance. THE DROP – The body, led by the hips, moves down and out, pushing and resisting against the windward rail with equally weighted feet. THE PUSH – Push through the toes.

LIFT AND LOCK or Straight 7
A narrow hand spread, tighten torso/stomach by lifting and locking hips. Pushing through the toes will help trim the board.

Session 4

HARNESS

Aim
To get students to hook into the harness lines and commit weight to the rig while running through the Formula to maintain a suitable sailing line.

Objectives
By the end of this session students should be able to:
- Control 'power' in and out of the harness.
- Take the weight off their arms.
- Use their 'stance' range for board and rig control.

Group Dynamics
This session should be split into two parts:
- Different harnesses available and the correct set up of harness lines.
- The use of the harness.
  The mechanics of using the harness are simple so concentrate on the use of the Formula to maintain sailing line, board speed and power control in and out of the harness.

Start with a session on different harnesses and the correct set up of harness lines. Follow it with a simulator demonstration on how to use the harness and apply areas of the Formula to encourage correct technique. Depending on group size and weather conditions, it may be appropriate to get the students to try the technique on the simulator before going afloat.

Information to be Covered
- Types of harness.
- Set up of harness lines.
- Hooking in and out.
- Use of sailing line.
- Stance range.
- During this session encourage the use of larger sails.
- Experiment with sailing line to control power and bring rig closer to body. Practise hooking in while using the Formula.

Learner Support Material
G51 – RYA Intermediate Windsurfing
Intermediate Coaching Notes (www.ryatraining.org/runningcourses/instructors/instructorresources)

Session 5

FOOTSTRAPS

Aim
To introduce the technique, working towards the use of foot straps without losing speed or control, while holding a comfortable course.

Objectives
By the end of this session, students should: Have the knowledge of, or be able to use the front and back footstraps maintaining a comfortable sailing line whilst using key elements of the Formula. Concentrate specifically on the counter balance element.

Group Dynamics
A good way to run this session, is to split it into two parts:
* The correct set up of footstraps.
* The mechanics of getting into the foot straps. This is simple so concentrate on effective coaching, helping them to maintain a good sailing direction, speed and power control to get into the straps. Use the simulator and an on water session. All areas of the Formula can be used here.

This session should start with a look at strap set up, followed by a simulator session and then on to the water. On water sessions will require enough wind to plane. However, if the wind is too light, a lot of valuable information can still be covered.

Information to be Covered
* Position and set up of straps (see equipment section page 133).
* Balance, weight transfer.
* Counter balance and Formula dynamics.
* Early planing and control of course direction.

Coaching Notes
A broad reach can encourage early planing and close reaching in stronger winds, to aid control.

Learner Support Material
G51 – RYA Intermediate Windsurfing
Intermediate Coaching Notes (www.rya.org.uk)

Session 6

BLASTING CONTROL

Aim
To show how the Formula can be used to improve board and rig control in a variety of conditions, increase acceleration and board control.

Objectives
By the end of this session, students should know how to adapt their stance to suit different wind and water conditions by using their full stance range.

Group Dynamics
This session is instructor led around the simulator and with on the water demos followed by student trials with regular feed back.

Start with a short recap on stance and stance range before going into the specific Formula use to maintain control at speed. This should be a short session if conditions on the water are good. You should cover light and strong wind control. Use simulator based scenarios for fault analysis and offer a Q and A opportunity for students to raise questions. On the water you should concentrate on sailing course and stance range to promote control.

Information to be Covered
- Use of the Formula while blasting, acceleration and board control through the stance range.

Coaching Notes
If conditions on the water don't allow the students to blast properly it is probably more beneficial to spend more time on the simulator with students having a go and asking questions.

Learner Support Material
G51 – RYA Intermediate Windsurfing
Intermediate Coaching Notes (www.rya.org.uk)

Coaches' Corner - Key terms in Blasting Control:

DROP AND DIG
A dynamic stance. THE DROP – The body, led by the hips, moves down and out, pushing and resisting against the windward rail with equally weighted feet. THE DIG – Drive through the heels.

DROP AND PUSH
A dynamic stance. THE DROP – The body, led by the hips, moves down and out, pushing and resisting against the windward rail with equally weighted feet. THE PUSH – Push through the toes.

LIFT AND LOCK or Straight 7
A narrow hand spread, tighten torso/stomach by lifting and locking hips. Pushing through the toes will help trim the board.

Session 7

STEERING

Aim
To introduce the concept of counter balance and improve stance to suit different conditions while changing direction.

Objectives
By the end of this session, students should be able to effectively change the board's direction using their vision and counter balance.

Group Dynamics
This session is split between the simulator and the water. It should include instructor demos afloat and student practice on the water, with the instructor giving continual feedback.

This steering session should concentrate on changing direction to alter course, or to avoid an obstacle, however, it will also form the basics of steering into and out of a tack or gybe. Keep this in mind for the tacking/gybing session.

While concentrating on vision and counter balance, remember to check all other areas of the Formula as you go through. Your session should cover steering in and out of the harness and footstraps, and will work well regardless of the conditions.

Information to be Covered
- Trim, counter balance and stance are key.
- Using the Formula for non-planing steering, up and downwind.
- Using the Formula for planing steering, up and downwind.

Coaching Notes
Remember this session is the forerunner to all transitions.

Learner Support Material
G51 – RYA Intermediate Windsurfing
Intermediate Coaching Notes (www.rya.org.uk)

> **Coaches' Corner – Key terms in Steering:**
>
> DROP AND DIG
> A dynamic stance. THE DROP – The body, led by the hips, moves down and out, pushing and resisting against the windward rail with equally weighted feet. THE DIG – Drive through the heels.

Session 8

TACKING

Aim
To increase the speed and effectiveness of the students' tacking ability.

Objectives
By the end of this session, students should be able to use the Formula for faster, and more effective tacking in a range of conditions.

Group Dynamics
This session should be split between land and water. The time split will depend on the ability of the group and the on water conditions. A good understanding of the skills is required before going afloat, but remember there is no substitute to going afloat. This session should focus on how our vision, counter balance and foot work create the tack. A good land demo with clear group understanding is vital. This can be achieved with dry land practice followed by on water exercises and instructor feedback.

The tack can be broken down in many ways. One particularly effective way is delivered in three sections: entry, mid and exit.

Information to be Covered
- Steering upwind and downwind.
- Foot work.
    'Shifting and switching' (see page 110).
    Drop and dig.
    Drop and push.
- Counter balance.
- Dynamic tacking.

Equipment Resources Required
- Rig/board without fin to be used on land.
- Suitable equipment to go afloat.

Learner Support Material
G51 – RYA Intermediate Windsurfing
Intermediate Coaching Notes (www.rya.org.uk)

Coaches' Corner – Key terms in Tacking:

DROP AND DIG

A dynamic stance. THE DROP – The body, led by the hips, moves down and out, pushing and resisting against the windward rail with equally weighted feet. THE DIG – Drive through the heels.

DROP AND PUSH

A dynamic stance. THE DROP – The body, led by the hips, moves down and out, pushing and resisting against the windward rail with equally weighted feet. THE PUSH – Push through the toes.

LIFT AND LOCK or Straight 7

A narrow hand spread, tighten torso/stomach by lifting and locking hips. Pushing through the toes will help trim the board.

Standard Clinic 1

BEACHSTARTS

Aim
To introduce the students to improved launching and landing skills, leading ultimately onto the waterstart.

Linking this session to other on water skills will lead to good board control and, perhaps, deep water beachstarts, depending on ability.

Objectives
By the end of this session the students should:
- Be able to launch without the need to uphaul their rig.
- Understand the concept of 'slide and guide' to clear the rig from the water, and the 'rig twister' to apply the correct balance and power in order to control their board and rig.

Group Dynamics
This session could be run as part of an intermediate course, or as a specific session/clinic. It could be run as a one to one or group session. This session requires some specific launching site requirements. Check to make sure that you have sufficient water depth for the fins that you are using and that the water depth does not drop off too quickly. This session can start with an instructor demo introducing the beachstart on the shore or on the water, followed by student practice and feedback from the instructor.

When initially introducing beachstarting to a group of students ensure a large launching area is available, with space between each student, especially in stronger winds. Smaller fins can also be used where waters are shallow.

Information to be Covered
- Light wind, strong wind.
- Shallow water big fin.
- Deep water.
- Rig elevation 'sliding and gliding'.
- Combining balance and power 'rig twisting'.
- Specific vision and trim 'nose over toes'.

Exercises or Follow-up Work
This session can be linked with other skills that require the student to repeatedly return to the shore and re-launch. Your students are therefore continually practising beachstarts while improving other skills.

Learner Support Material
G51 – RYA Intermediate Windsurfing
Intermediate Coaching Notes (www.rya.org.uk)

Coaches' Corner – Key terms in Beachstarts:

RIG ELEVATION – Sliding the mast to windward as you elevate the rig above your head.

RIG TWISTING – Creating lift from the rig by thrusting the front arm up and forwards as the back hand pulls the boom in above your head.

NOSE OVER TOES – Bending the back leg and rolling the head inboard below the boom towards the mast base.

Standard Clinic 2

THE NON-PLANING CARVE GYBE

Aim
To introduce the student to a simple gybe that can be used in non-planing conditions and planing conditions. It forms the platform for learning the Planing Carve Gybe.

Objectives
By the end of this session, students should be able to turn the board round by gybing and breaking down the skill. Try using vision, counter balance, stance and footwork, Shift and Switch and the Rig Rotator to help with key areas.

Group Dynamics
This session could be run as part of an intermediate course or as a specific session/clinic. It could be run as a one to one or group session. Start with dry land simulation of gybing followed by on water exercises and instructor feedback.

Although time will need to be spent ashore learning the basic technique, it is important to maximise the time on the water. Once on the water, start the session with a demonstration and break the skills down into different sections, perhaps entry, mid and exit, or hand and footwork etc.

Resources Required
- Rig/board without fin to be used on land.

Information to be Covered
- Rig rotator.
- Shifting and switching.
- Progression from non-planing to planing skills.
- Drop and push.

Coaching Notes
In the early stages, concentrate on one skill at a time. See the intermediate coaching notes, G51 Intermediate Handbook, for further breakdown and delivery.

Learner Support Material
G51 – RYA Intermediate Windsurfing
Intermediate Coaching Notes (www.rya.org.uk)

Coaches' Corner – Key terms in the Non-planing Carve Gybe:

DROP AND DIG

A dynamic stance. THE DROP – The body, led by the hips, moves down and out, pushing and resisting against the windward rail with equally weighted feet. THE DIG – Drive through the heels.

DROP AND PUSH

A dynamic stance. THE DROP – The body, led by the hips, moves down and out, pushing and resisting against the windward rail with equally weighted feet. THE PUSH – Push through the toes.

SHIFTING AND SWITCHING

A movement of the feet during both the tacking and gybing sequence.

RIG ROTATOR

During the gybe the mast goes through a specific action: a rotation downwind, back towards the tail and then forward in one smooth action.

Advanced Windsurfing Teaching System

As seen in the Intermediate section, the strength of the Fastfwd coaching method is that essential skills and objectives are introduced very early on in students' learning the sport. In advanced coaching we continue to refer to, use and improve on these basic, yet defining, skills.

Someone may be able to plane in the harness and footstraps on a larger volume board in marginal winds. However they will need to continue to develop each element in the Formula to enable them to deal with stronger winds, more challenging conditions and lower volume boards. Essentially we are using identical skills and objectives learnt in the intermediate section to help us become more efficient and effective in their application.

The advanced clinics are a seamless continuation from the intermediate clinics. Beachstarts progress to become waterstarts and the non-planing carve gybe transfers to the carve gybe. We encourage the use of the pre-learned skills and coaching concepts, ensuring swift and easy progression.

Despite the higher level of the course and the students' objectives, it remains vital to use the Formula and its accompanying skills.

As advanced instructors, this enables us to isolate and perfect the defining skills that really make the difference on the water. As we know progression to higher levels is so often down to developing and re-focusing the skills and techniques that students already have.

Equally, you'll probably find that more advanced windsurfers have a better understanding of our sport. Often progress has been hampered by bad habits, while good habits have not been fully applied. It is common for people to imagine that there must be something more complicated that needs to be learnt to become a better windsurfer. In reality, the best windsurfers are just really good at the basics. It's all about emphasizing those basics, all of which are in the Fastfwd Formula and the transitional skills:

- A flatter board for early planing.
- More weight in the harness or curl on the toes in stronger winds.
- Fully shifting the hips and bending the knees in the gybe.

Greater board speeds give students less time to think and, possibly, a more challenging coaching environment. Below are three major considerations for advanced instructors and coaches to think about:

- Simplify your delivery. Where possible summarize your coaching suggestions and break moves or objectives down into the key parts. On the water, focus on one skill or objective at a time.
- Always try to sail on your students' equipment so you can make sure that things such as harness line set up are correct. Fatigue and board handling problems are vastly exaggerated in stronger winds when gear isn't set up properly.
- Finally, and probably the most important message for Advanced coaching is accentuation of, and even greater commitment to, the key elements and skills within the Formula and transitions.

CONTENT

Advanced Delivery

Advanced getting going/harness/footstraps & blasting control

Blasting control additions

- Spin out.
- Head upwind.
- Upwind off the plane.
- Strong wind uphaul.

Intermediate to Advanced Clinics

Waterstart (incorporating intermediate beachstart)

Carve Gybe (incorporating Non-Planing Carve Gybe)

Additional Advanced Clinics

Gybe Variations

Bump & Jump

Session 1

BLASTING CONTROL – (PROGRESSION FROM INTERMEDIATE SESSION, PAGE 102)

Aim

The following themed skills are covered in the Intermediate Blasting Control section (see page 102). However they are worth highlighting and incorporating into your coaching when working with students in more challenging conditions or on lower volume boards.

Objectives

The following skills are chosen for their particular usefulness when encountering stronger winds, greater speeds and more response from the equipment in use. They reinforce the objectives of certain elements in the Formula but, most importantly, they help the student create control and greater confidence in more advanced situations:

- Head upwind for control.
- Sailing upwind off the plane.
- Uphauling on short boards or in strong winds.

You will see how vision and sailing line play a huge role in getting sorted in advanced situations!

Information to be Covered

In addition to the information above and that contained in the Intermediate Coaching Notes, due to higher speeds, chop and smaller fins, Spin Out in the context of the following areas should also be discussed:

- Equipment setup.
- Trim, balance, power, stance.

Learner Support Material

G51 – RYA Intermediate Windsurfing
G52 – RYA Advanced Windsurfing
Intermediate and Advanced Coaching Notes, available from: www.rya.org.uk

---

Coaches' Corner – Key terms in Blasting Control

DROP AND DIG
A dynamic stance. THE DROP – The body, led by the hips, moves down and out, pushing and resisting against the windward rail with equally weighted feet. THE DIG – Drive through the heels.

DROP AND PUSH
A dynamic stance. THE DROP – The body, led by the hips, moves down and out, pushing and resisting against the windward rail with equally weighted feet. THE PUSH – Push through the toes.

LIFT AND LOCK or Straight 7
A narrow hand spread, tighten torso/stomach by lifting and locking hips. Pushing through the toes will help trim the board.

Session 2

HEAD UPWIND (PROGRESSION FROM INTERMEDIATE SESSION, PAGES 104-105)

Aim
Key Formula elements: Vision
To instil the importance of heading upwind to gain control, which should have been established from an early stage in your students' windsurfing careers. It is vital to make this 'routine' in stronger or marginal planing conditions, on lower volume boards.

Objectives
By the end of the session/course the students should have a greater knowledge or ideally, experience of taking the board upwind. They should be able to get the board and rig settled in a number of different situations.

Group Dynamics
Use any of the following situations to demonstrate the importance of heading upwind to establish control, save energy and improve safety in stronger winds. Provide your students with practical demonstrations, and linking back to vision and the importance of our sailing line.
- Setting up and coming up onto the board during a beach or waterstart.
- Encourage heading upwind whenever off the plane.
- Uphauling in planing winds or on lower volume boards.
- Prior to getting going, harnessing and footstraps.
- Any situation when trying to reduce speed and/or gain control.
- In over-powered or challenging situations when setting up for tacks, gybes, chop hops, body drags or jumping waves.

Coaching Notes
Two key areas to help coach these skills:
- Sailing upwind off the plane.
- Strong wind or low volume uphaul.

Learner Support Material
G51 – RYA Intermediate Windsurfing
G52 – RYA Advanced Windsurfing
Intermediate and Advanced Coaching Notes, available from: www.rya.org.uk

Coaches' Corner – Key terms in Steering

DROP AND DIG

A dynamic stance. THE DROP – The body, led by the hips, moves down and out, pushing and resisting against the windward rail with equally weighted feet. THE DIG – Drive through the heels.

DROP AND PUSH

A dynamic stance. THE DROP – The body, led by the hips, moves down and out, pushing and resisting against the windward rail with equally weighted feet. THE PUSH – Push through the toes.

Session 3

UPWIND OFF THE PLANE (PROGRESSION FROM INTERMEDIATE)

Aim
To sail upwind without a daggerboard.
Key Formula elements: Vision, trim and counter balance

Objectives
By the end of the session the students should be able to sail upwind, off the plane in non-planing or planing conditions, on a board without a daggerboard.

Group Dynamics
Show the importance of both vision and trim by setting up practical demos followed by a group session with very short runs.

Information to be Covered
- Vision, Trim, Balance, Power and Stance.

Coaching notes
Demonstrate how heading and tracking slowly upwind out of the harness gets them upwind before bearing away. Show how heading upwind off the plane is far more productive and less tiring than sailing across the wind, half in and out of the harness while trying to get going. With practice it is possible to sail upwind off the plane using a harness.

Show how little effort is required, even in very strong winds or on very low volume boards.

Learner Support Material
G51 – RYA Intermediate Windsurfing
G52 – RYA Advanced Windsurfing
Intermediate and Advanced Coaching Notes, available from: www.rya.org.uk

---

Coaches' Corner – Key terms in Steering

DROP AND DIG
A dynamic stance. THE DROP – The body, led by the hips, moves down and out, pushing and resisting against the windward rail with equally weighted feet. THE DIG – Drive through the heels.

Session 4

STRONG WIND OR LOW VOLUME BOARD UPHAULING

Aim
To dramatically increase ease, and reduce the fatigue, of uphauling in planing winds or on lower volume boards. Once again reinforcing the key skill of heading upwind in difficult situations.
Key Formula elements: Vision, trim and counter balance

Objectives
By the end of the session the students should be able to:
- Uphaul by facing the board towards the wind rather than across the wind.
- Allow the rig to come from the back of the board towards the front, making it easier to apply power, get going and remain balanced in challenging situations.

Group Dynamics
- This exercise can be run as a light wind session linked with safety, or as a demo when taking non-waterstarting students out in planing winds. It is particularly useful for:
- Uphauling in planing winds or on choppy waters.
- Uphauling on lower volume boards if the wind has suddenly dropped.

Information to be Covered
Developing existing uphauling technique with the emphasis on heading and staying upwind, during and after uphauling.
- Vision, Trim, Balance, Power and Stance (Especially – Super 7 Drop and Push).

Coaching Notes
It is important to use existing uphauling skills, while ensuring that during and after the final rig release the rig is back, the body is reasonably far forward and the board is pointing as close into the wind as possible.

This technique reduces wobble. Students will find it easier to balance and sheet in on a lower volume board, in rough water or in stronger winds.

Learner Support Material
G51 – RYA Intermediate Windsurfing
G52 – RYA Advanced Windsurfing
Intermediate and Advanced Coaching Notes, available from: www.rya.org.uk

Standard Advanced Clinic 1

WATERSTART

Aim
To waterstart in deep water.

Beachstarts and waterstarts rely on a sequence of specific mechanical skills that sit slightly outside our regular windsurfing actions. It is important to introduce the benefits of waterstarting as early as possible and to encourage students to start learning regardless of their current level. If you have the environment and conditions to coach waterstarting, it is possible to see students mastering waterstarts even before they can plane in the harness and footstraps properly. This enables the technique to be introduced alongside the essential skills for windsurfing, and build confidence when sailing lower volume boards.

Objectives
By the end of this session, the students should be able to:
- Fly the rig without standing on the ground.
- Correctly position the board and rig.
- Create lift from the rig to help bring themselves towards and up onto the board.
- Understand the correct body position to maximize the rig's lift.

Group Dynamics
This session can be run as part of an advanced course or as a specific session or clinic, either in a one to one or group session. To aid simplicity waterstarting exercises could be linked with sailing upwind off the plane for a short distance, before dropping down into the water. Keeping students upwind and close to the shore counteracts the tendency to drift downwind when learning to waterstart.

Try to find progressively deeper water so that students can practice each of the skills without their feet touching the ground.

Information to be Covered
The beachstarting skills lead on to learning the waterstart. Due to the board and rig orientation being in deeper water, we need to teach how to get everything correctly placed before making this essentially a higher wind move.

Break the move down into these four specific skills:

- Board and rig orientation in deeper water.
- Rig elevation – 'sliding and gliding' the rig to clear it from the water.
- Generating lift – 'rig twisting' and orientation using balance and power.
- Specific vision – 'nose over toes' to minimise body weight on the rig.

Exercises or Follow-up Work

Each of the waterstart skills can be taught as separate exercises to build up muscle memory and reduce fatigue. If teaching beachstarting, start your delivery from the rig elevation section – from a standing rather than deep water position.

Learner Support Material

G51 – RYA Intermediate Windsurfing, G52 – RYA Advanced Windsurfing
Intermediate and Advanced Coaching Notes, available from: www.rya.org.uk

Coaches' Corner – Key terms in Waterstart

SLIDE AND GLIDE – Taking the mast across, over the head and as far to windward as possible.

RIG TWISTING – Creating lift from the rig, by thrusting the front arm up and forwards as the back hand pulls the boom in above your head.

NOSE OVER TOES – An action of bending the back leg and rolling the head inboard below the boom towards the mast base.

Standard Advanced Clinic 2

PLANING CARVE GYBE

Aim
To develop the non-plaing carve gybe into the planing carve gybe.

Planing carve gybes are one of the most exciting, rewarding and yet commonly over-complicated aspects of windsurfing. By using Fastfwd we develop the skills and specifics learnt during the non-planing carve gybe to form a more fluid turn in planing conditions.

Objectives
By the end of this session, students should be able to:
- Set up, unhook and control the entry into the gybe.
- Apply ample pressure to the inside rail to create the carving action.
- 'Shift and switch' the feet while counter-balancing and controlling the rig.
- Time the rig release to carry out the rig rotator.
- Be able to turn the board round by gybing and breaking down the skill.

Group Dynamics
This session could be run as part of an advanced course or specific session or clinic, and as a one to one or group session. Start with a short dry land demonstration of a particular section, followed by either light or strong wind demonstration and exercises, reinforced with instructor feedback.

Information to be Covered
Essentially carve gybing comes down to developing and stressing the importance of:
- Vision.
- Continually counter balancing the movement of the rig.
- Super 7 'drop and push' stance for higher speed set ups and exits.
- Steering the board through the turn.

Then, like the non-planing carve gybes, adding two vital specific skills:
- 'Shifting and switching' to position the body, moving the hips and switching the feet mid-gybe.
- Rig rotator to control the rig's release, movement and ease of sheeting in again.

Due to the speed and co-ordination required, it is impossible to remember a long series of actions, so simplify your delivery: Try teaching the gybe in three sections incorporating vision and counter balance throughout. Add extra detail for individual requirements or fault diagnosis:
- ENTRY – Super 7 set up for unhooking and gybe entry.
- MID – Shifting and switching for the hip and foot movement while carving.
- EXIT – Rig rotator to control the rig change and super 7 once again for gybe exit.

The planing carve gybe continues to develop the skills of the non-planing carve gybe.

However three factors that make the planing carve gybe are a little more dynamic:

- ENTRY – The super 7 set up before and after unhooking starts from a speedier, more outboard and committed position.
- MID – Increased pressure and commitment is applied to the inside carving rail before, during and even after shifting and switching the feet mid gybe.
- EXIT – Finally, the rig is not leant out of the turn so much and it is released slightly earlier due to the extra turning speed of the board.

When teaching a non-planing carve gybe as a training exercise in lighter winds, the major differences are:

- Start from a less outboard position.
- Less pressure on the inside rail.
- The rig is leant out of the turn more and released a little later.

Apart from those slight changes, all the gybing skills have a smooth progression.

Resources Required

- A full understanding and good delivery of the key/core skills.
- A finless board as a simulator (ideally with a powered up rig).
- Non-planing carve gybe on water exercises.

Learner Support Material

G51 – RYA Intermediate Windsurfing
G52 – RYA Advanced Windsurfing
Intermediate and Advanced Coaching Notes, available from: www.rya.org.uk

Coaches' Corner – Key terms in Planing Carve Gybe:

DROP AND DIG – A dynamic stance. THE DROP – The body, led by the hips, moves down and out, pushing and resisting against the windward rail with equally weighted feet. THE DIG – Drive through the heels.

DROP AND PUSH – A dynamic stance. THE DROP – The body, led by the hips, moves down and out, pushing and resisting against the windward rail with equally weighted feet. THE PUSH - Push through the toes.

SHIFT AND SWITCH – A movement of the feet during both the tacking and gybing sequence.

RIG ROTATOR – During the gybe the mast goes through a specific action – a rotation downwind, back towards the tail and then forward in one smooth action.

Standard Advanced Clinic 3

PLANING CARVE SKILLS (ADVANCED GYBING TECHNIQUE)

Over the years gybing has evolved, leaving confusion about styles and concepts. The main gybe outlined in the intermediate and advanced coaching methods is a proven, versatile method. Below are the different styles of gybes and how they differ from our recommended gybe. By varying one major element from the Fastfwd Formula – counter balance – it will enable you to change the style of gybe.

STEP GYBE
A gybe where the feet are switched before the rig is rotated.

STRAP-TO-STRAP
Also known as a 'classic' or 'wave board' gybe.

SLAM GYBE
Also known as 'pivot', 'chicken' or 'survival' gybe! A more extreme example of the stronger wind step gybe.

SLALOM/LAYDOWN
This originates from the step gybe camp, where the feet are changed before the rig. The objective is to over sheet the rig, and get more weight onto the inside rail. To enable this to happen there is a fundamental change in how we counter balance.

Resources Required
- A full understanding and good delivery of the key/core skills.
- A finless board as a simulator (ideally with a powered up rig).
- Non-planing carve gybe on water exercises.

Learner Support Material
G51 – RYA Intermediate Windsurfing
G52 – RYA Advanced Windsurfing
Intermediate and Advanced Coaching Notes, available from: www.rya.org.uk

Standard Advanced Clinic 4

BUMP & JUMP

Aim
Chop hop and jumping. Basically, 'Air time!'

Objectives
By the end of this session, students should be able to:
- Set up and unhook - reversing the Formula for take off.
- Apply ample pressure to the tail from an elevated sailing position.
- Control the flight of board by re-establishing the Formula.
- Land safely, ideally maintaining speed.

Group Dynamics
This session could be run as part of an advanced course, as a specific session or clinic or as a one to one or group session.

Information to be Covered
- Importance of spotting troughs of wavelets and changing sailing line.
- Temporarily reversing each element in the Formula to induce take off (apart from vision).
- Performing an exaggerated super 7 mid flight, then re-establishing the Formula for landing.
- Coping with unwanted jumps.

Coaching Notes
- It is important to stress that jumping is NOT about trying to 'jump' the board while in a sailing position. It is vital to momentarily change the sailing position and work on the timing of pushing down in the trough, rather than looking for a wave to jump off.
- If possible, hold a board with hands in the straps on the shore. Demonstrate how extra lift is generated when the board is turned towards the wind 5-15 degrees, and the tail is depressed, rather than being held flat across the wind and trying to pull the board up.

Learner Support Material
G51 – RYA Intermediate Windsurfing
G52 – RYA Advanced Windsurfing
Intermediate and Advanced Coaching Notes, available from: www.rya.org.uk

Start Racing Sessions

The next two sessions are taken from the Racing Instructor Manual, resources specifically designed to act as a companion to the Racing Instructor Course. It helps you deliver Start Racing courses and Team15 training sessions.

Each exercise can be incorporated in your session, whether adult or junior. You don't have to be a Racing Instructor to deliver them, and these simple exercises are a fantastic opportunity to introduce the concept of racing into your general session as a fun alternative.

The RYA racing scheme, along with the pathway, provides participants with high potential an easy route to the top of the sport. While the ladder is in place to allow talented sailors to progress rapidly to the top of the sport, to make this work effectively, it is essential we introduce and attract as many participants as possible to windsurfing.

For individuals to stay interested in windsurfing the sport must be made fun and improvement must be recognised. Racing is an ideal way of keeping the sport fun, especially for juniors, increasing the rate of improvement and providing goals to strive towards.

It is therefore extremely important at this level of involvement that racing is dealt with using a soft approach. Racing should not be seen as a high-pressure, aggressive side to the sport. Instead, it should be a way of increasing the fun factor and improving the learning curve.

In summary, the scheme has been designed to improve the numbers and retention of participants within windsurfing by making the sport more fun and less intimidating. The route is then established for participants to progress up a ladder of success with those with most potential making it to the very top level of our sport – Olympic Gold medals and world titles. If you enjoy delivering the exercises we have outlined, or fancy furthering your skill and getting involved with the teaching of the racing scheme, why not take the leap and look into becoming a Racing Instructor? Pages 31-32 and page 144 provide further details.

Session 1

STARTING

It is estimated that this topic will take approximately three on the water sessions to complete. The key factor is to ensure that participants have adequate board handling skills to be right on the start line at the go.

Log book sections covered:	Getting near the start line on the gun.
	Stopping and holding position.
Estimated time to cover topic:	3 x 45 min on water sessions.
Ideal conditions:	4-15 knots.
Relevant sessions:	10,11,12.

Coach Preparation
It was established in 'RACING KNOWLEDGE – Starting' that the most important factor in achieving a good start at this level of participation, is to be on the start line at the go. To achieve this it was recommended that participants should be on the line (or at least very near to it) with at least 45 seconds to the start, and have the board handling skills to stay there. Therefore, this topic is aimed at developing board handling skills and familiarisation with basic start routines and timing.

Board Handling Skills
The two main skills necessary on a start line are:
1   Tight radius tacking and gybing.
2   Holding station.
Tight radius tacking and gybing should already have been dealt with in 'TURNING TECHNIQUES – Faster tacks and gybes'.

Holding Station
It was established in 'RACING KNOWLEDGE – Starting' that the easiest way to reverse a board is to point it across the wind with the sail sheeted out. This position is basically the secure position that was taught at stage 1, but serves the purpose well!

Additional Information
W3 Racing Instructors Manual
The Winning Streak DVD

Session Delivery
It is aimed to cover this topic in three on the water sessions. The sessions are structured in a way that will improve the participants' board handling skills and their confidence of being in the starting area.

Session 2

TACTICS AND STRATEGY

The aim of this session is to give participants who can already sail around a course guidance how to keep clear wind

Log book sections covered:	Keeping clear wind.
Estimated time to cover topic:	40 min on water session.
Ideal conditions:	4-15 knots.
Relevant session/s:	19.

Coach Preparation

It is essential that racers have an awareness of when they are in dirty wind. This can seem simple but when in the thick of competition, the obvious can be easily missed. By running a session where sailors have to distinguish when they are in dirty wind and when they have escaped it, will help them when racing.

A really good exercise is to put sailors into pairs to sail around a small course. They have to take turns at being either covered or covering the other sailor. If they are the covered sailor, they should try to escape the cover by tacking, gybing or sailing higher or lower than their opponent.

It is crucial that the sailors understand that keeping clear air is the number one priority. This is often the cause of many bad racers complaining about being slow. Often slowness is mistaken for sailing in less wind than other racers!

Additional Information

W3 – Racing Instructors Manual
The Winning Streak DVD

Session Delivery

It is aimed to cover this topic in one session. Once participants become aware of the effect of dirty wind it will help them when making race decisions and evaluate performance. The key is to help create an understanding of the effect of dirty wind, and to ensure sailors see it as a priority.

Theory Session Aids

Introduction

This section is a resource for all instructors from Start to Advanced, providing a guide to what you should teach your students at the various stages of their progression through the scheme. Remember, covering theory within our sessions is essential to our students being safe and getting the most out of their windsurfing.

When planning your theory sessions, use a method that will be most effective in helping your students learn and retain information. Delivering theory during practical sessions or making sessions as real as possible can aid delivery.

RYA Windsurfing publications that should be used in conjunction are:
G47 – RYA National Windsurfing Scheme Syllabus & Logbook
W1 – RYA Youth Windsurfing Scheme Syllabus & Logbook
G49 – RYA Start Windsurfing
G51 – RYA Intermediate Windsurfing
G52 – RYA Advanced Windsurfing
Theory notes are available on the RYA website.

Other resources produced by the RYA covering specific areas will increase your own knowledge of a particular subject, if limited. A list of suggested publications can be found within each theory section as well as on page 156.

Tides

What to teach our students

Aim
The purpose of this section is to enable students to enjoy windsurfing and be safe at a
tidal location.

It is important not to overload your students with information. Use the guide below to help
cover the appropriate information, assisting their understanding and progression, according to
their ability level.

Information to be Covered
START
- What a tide is.
- What causes tides.
- Daily movement: horizontal and vertical.
- Sources.
- Tide timetable.
- How tides affect us and a good time to go out.
- Basic buoyage systems.

INTERMEDIATE
- Monthly Tides – Springs and Neaps.
- Tidal range and tidal streams – Rule of twelfths etc.
- Effects of tidal streams and their direction – wind against, wind with, depth.

ADVANCED
- Tidal variations – yearly cycles of tide.
- Beach gradient.
- Obstruction to flow – races, overfalls etc.
- Rip tides.

Learning Support Material
- RYA Windsurfing publications; G47 – RYA National Windsurfing Scheme Syllabus &
  Logbook, W1 – RYA Youth Windsurfing Scheme Syllabus & Logbook, G49 – RYA Start
  Windsurfing, G51 – RYA Intermediate Windsurfing, G52 – RYA Advanced Windsurfing.
- The RYA publishes other resources covering specific areas, if your own knowledge of a
  particular subject is limited. We have made suggestions on page 156 for other books
  you may find useful.

Weather

What to teach our students

Aim

The purpose of this section is to help our students understand the fundamentals behind wind and weather. This includes the ability to interpret a forecast, or simply to read the visual signs all around us, enabling them to make an informed decision on where and when to go windsurfing in safety.

The UK and other windsurfing destinations around the world are fantastic places for seeing and experiencing the effects of wind and weather. As an instructor, take advantage of this fact – use visual means and examples to help put this subject into context, just as with any classroom based theory session.

Wind and weather is a large topic. Be careful to keep it simple, interesting and relevant to the ability of the students.

Information to be Covered
START
- Wind direction – compass and shore line.
- Wind Strength – Beaufort Scale.
- Source and types – understanding and interpreting.
- Backing and veering.

INTERMEDIATE
- Weather systems – The creation of, and expected conditions within, a high and low pressure system.
- Synoptic charts – understanding, symbols and fronts.
- Local effects – seas and land breezes.

ADVANCED
- Passage of a depression.
- Local effects.
- Anabatic and Katabatic winds.

Learning Support Material
- RYA Windsurfing publications; G47 – RYA National Windsurfing Scheme Syllabus & Logbook, W1 – RYA Youth Windsurfing Scheme Syllabus & Logbook, G49 – RYA Start Windsurfing, G51 – RYA Intermediate Windsurfing, G52 – RYA Advanced Windsurfing.
- The RYA publishes other resources covering specific areas if your own knowledge of a particular subject is limited. We have made suggestions on page 156 for other books you may find useful.

Safety

Aim

The purpose of this section is to give students an appreciation of the risks involved in windsurfing and how to minimise those risks, while maintaining maximum enjoyment of the sport. Any presentation on safety should be relevant to students' ability levels and should also take into consideration their ambitions for the near future (i.e. sailing at a coastal location/ stronger winds etc).

Split the topic into various elements. Think carefully about when it would be appropriate to introduce certain bits of information on this subject to students so as to assist their understanding and progression relevant to their ability level.

Beware of making the topic seem daunting and/or dull. Safety issues, especially topics such as self rescue, can be made very enjoyable with a little imagination and forward planning, and result in students remembering the information and feeling confident to utilise it when necessary.

Instructor Safety Equipment

Instructors are responsible for the safety of their group as well as themselves. Therefore, in addition to general safety items, depending on the instructional environment additional items may be carried such as:

- A 4m length of floating rope, for the purpose of towing one board from another. Ideally a towline should be slightly stretchy to absorb shock.
- A knife: A lockable blade with a serrated cutting edge is very useful for cutting away jammed or tangled ropes.
- A whistle.
- Dayglo flag.

Additional equipment easily accessible to us should be such items as; a first aid kit, radio/ mobile phone etc. This may be carried on your person or in accompanying safety boat, but should be in an easily accessible place ashore.

For a full list and guidance of safety equipment required at an RYA recognised training centre refer to:

- G16 – RYA Safety Boat Handbook.
- UK and Overseas Standards for an RYA Training Centre.

Information to be Covered

START

- 7 common senses, Check, Check, Check.
- Avoiding other craft – basic rules of the road.
- Choosing a safe sailing location – Wind direction to shore.
- Methods of self rescue.

INTERMEDIATE

- Self rescue on lower volume boards.
- Towing – behind.

ADVANCED

- Nature of a shore break.
- Dealing with equipment failure.
- Launching and landing in surf.
- Currents in surf – long shore drift and rights of way.

Learning Support Material

G47 – RYA National Windsurfing Scheme Syllabus & Logbook, W1 – RYA Youth Windsurfing Scheme Syllabus & Logbook, G49 – RYA Start Windsurfing, G51 – RYA Intermediate Windsurfing, G52 – RYA Advanced Windsurfing.

Sailing Theory

Aim

To give students an understanding of how the board and sail work, and some of the terms commonly used.

- Keep your teaching simple so that you don't confuse your students. If you don't understand it, your students won't either!
- Don't give too much information too soon.
- Use the guides to make sure you give the right level of detail for the course you are running.

Information to be Covered

START

- Commonly used terms.
- Centre of effort.
- Centre of lateral resistance.
- How a board steers.

INTERMEDIATE

- Lift – the creation of lift in a sail. Visual examples.
- Turbulent and laminar flow.
- Apparent wind.
- Points of sailing and dagger position.
- Fins and how a fin works, including lift and types of fins.
- Railing.

ADVANCED

- Leading edge.
- Sail Profile and twist.
- Fins: Different types, designs and their effect on performance.
- Spin out.

Learning Support Material

- G47 – RYA National Windsurfing Scheme Syllabus & Logbook, W1 – RYA Youth Windsurfing Scheme Syllabus & Logbook, G49 – RYA Start Windsurfing, G51 – RYA Intermediate Windsurfing, G52 – RYA Advanced Windsurfing.
- The RYA publishes other resources covering specific areas if your own knowledge of a particular subject is limited. We have made suggestions on page 156 for other books you may find useful.

Equipment

Aim

The purpose of the equipment section is to give our students the relevant information and knowledge so that they can select the right equipment for their needs and set it up correctly.

Having plenty of props and visual aids makes presentations on equipment more interesting, realistic and memorable!

As with all the other theory sections, use the guide below to help convey the appropriate information to students, assisting their understanding and progression according to their ability level.

Information to be Covered

START

- Wetsuits: basic characteristics, materials, styles and stitching.
- Other personal equipment and accessories.
- Parts of the board, fins.
- Parts of the rig and basic rigging.
- Buying your first board and rig.

INTERMEDIATE

- Personal equipment: harness (types, fit); wetsuits (types and materials).
- Types of boards: set up (footstraps and mastfoot).
- Rig components, materials (sail and mast).
- Types of sails (inc kids).
- Rigging and tuning: setting boom height, harness lines inc length and position.
- Fin types – shape, size in relation to sail.

ADVANCED

- Board design features and construction.
- Fin performance and profile, designs, material and position.
- Rig performance (inc: mast and boom) and advanced tuning of all components.

Learning Support Material

- G47 – RYA National Windsurfing Scheme Syllabus & Logbook, W1 – RYA Youth Windsurfing Scheme Syllabus & Logbook, G49 – RYA Start Windsurfing, G51 – RYA Intermediate Windsurfing, G52 – RYA Advanced Windsurfing.
- The RYA publishes other resources covering specific areas if your own knowledge of a particular subject is limited. We have made suggestions on page 156 for other books you may find useful.

Running RYA Instructor Training

Introduction

RYA instructor training is run on behalf of the RYA by appointed Trainers and Coaches at Recognised Training Centres across the UK and overseas, increasing accessibility to our training courses.

To ensure instructor training is run to the correct standard, each course must be authorised. If you wish to organise an RYA instructor course at your centre liaise with your Regional Development Officer, If your centre is overseas, please contact RYA Training direct.

Course guidance can be found within this book and relevant areas of the RYA Training website (www.rya.org.uk).

The following sections and information can be found within this chapter:

Instructor Training
Information on each type of instructor course that we hope will be both useful for both potential instructors and for RYA Trainers running these courses.

Qualification Log
Each instructor course taken should be logged and signed by the course trainer. This can be a useful proof of attendance should it ever be required.

Teaching Experience Log
It is a prerequisite for each windsurfing instructor course that a specific number of teaching hours are gained prior to progressing on to the next level.

Assistant Instructor Training

Duration: 20-25 hours
Run by RYA Senior Instructor

The training and assessment is conducted by the Principal or Chief Instructor who holds a valid RYA Senior Instructor Certificate.

The role of the Assistant Instructor is to assist qualified instructors to teach beginners courses up to and including the standard of Start Windsurfing in the National Windsurfing Scheme and Stage 2 in the Youth Windsurfing Scheme. Assistant Instructors should always work under the supervision of an RYA Windsurfing Senior Instructor, helping qualified RYA Instructors in the early stages of a group's learning. The training provided should be relevant to individuals interested in encouraging children and adults to learn to windsurf.

A Senior Windsurfing Instructor who also holds a Dinghy Instructor qualification or above, may apply for recognition, supervise both activities, and is eligible to run the Assistant Instructor training for both disciplines. For guidance on running Dinghy Assistant Instructor training please refer to G14 RYA National Sailing Scheme Instructor Handbook.

Course Information and Content
When providing the training, the Principal or Chief Instructor will have in their mind the role of the Assistant Instructor within their centre – helping qualified instructors and training should be run accordingly. Training may be given on a specific Assistant Instructor course over about 20 hours, or provided on a one-to-one basis over a longer period as on the job training. A suggested programme is below. A vast majority of the time should be spent afloat and on a simulator covering how to put across the various teaching points for each section of the basic teaching method.

As the Assistant Instructor qualification is centre specific, the training should relate directly to the work of that particular centre.

Assessment
Candidates should be assessed on their practical teaching ability with beginners. Successful candidates will have their logbook signed and be awarded an RYA Assistant Instructor Certificate by their Principal. This certificate is only valid at that centre for five years, although the certificate can be re-issued by the centre Principal. During this time it is recommended that candidates look towards training to become a fully qualified RYA instructor.

Assistant Instructor Programme (sample)

Evening	Day 1	Day 2
Welcome and introductions Role and qualities of an Assistant Instructor. Basic principles and instructor techniques.	The Start Windsurfing teaching method – W4a. Introduction to the simulator and siting.	Simulator work – Recapping Onshore 1 Onshore 2
	Simulator work - Onshore 1	On water 1 and 2 demos
	Safety briefing and awareness Personal skills sailing	Games
	On water 1 demos	Group control
	Equipment suitability	Coaching positioning
	Youth and adult scheme	Health and safety
		Child Protection
		Reporting to the SI
		Debriefs

Start Instructor Training

Duration: 5 days
Run by RYA Start Windsurfing Trainer

The structure of the RYA Start Windsurfing teaching method forms the basis for this instructor course. The teaching method has been developed over many years, providing a standardised method of instruction. This is an important part of ensuring RYA instruction broadly follows the same pattern in every training centre. This standardised method enables instructors to move from one centre to another teaching any part of the method. The progressive nature of the RYA schemes also enables students to move to different centres to develop their skills, with the centres knowing exactly what has been covered previously.

The Start Windsurfing Instructor, although responsible for teaching individuals and small groups, has not been assessed as competent to run a windsurfing centre and should always work under the supervision of an RYA Senior Instructor. Once qualified, a Start Windsurfing Instructor is qualified to teach taster sessions, Start Windsurfing Courses and Stage 1 and 2 of the Youth scheme.

It is recommended that, prior to the course, candidates are happy with their ability to windsurf to the minimum ever required of a confident Intermediate Non Planing sailor and the instructor skills assessment (required criteria outlined below). Evidence of the appropriate instructor sailing skills level should be conducted as a self assessment prior to the course, it may be advisable to seek assistance from a qualified intermediate instructor to ensure you are of the required standard. The course trainer may ask each candidate to demonstrate during the instructor course, that they have the board skills required to become an instructor.

The method is designed to be taught in a progressive manner with the instructor introducing, demonstrating and the students practising each step at a time, recapping as they progress and improve. The unique manner in which the method has been developed forms a platform for the continual development of all future windsurfing skills. The teaching method, Fastfwd, uses similar basics to develop specific skills and transitions.

The aim is to provide instructors with enough support to get students sailing safely on their own as soon as possible. Each skill is broken down into easy steps for both the instructor and the student to follow (See pages 77-95), with an end goal of the Start Windsurfing course, being a smooth, flowing combination of the movements taught using the method.

The section on Methods of teaching and coaching (pages 35-60), will help develop the ability to pass over the skills in a manner that all students can learn and understand.

Course Content

During the Start Windsurfing course a number of different modules will be covered, ensuring sufficient knowledge is gained to teach under the supervision of a Senior Instructor.

Background Knowledge
- RYA schemes: The structure of the National and Youth Windsurfing Scheme, RYA initiatives and basic RYA structure.
- Safeguarding, child protection, health & safety and cold water shock.

Course Management
- Course structure, content and preparation.
- Equipment and simulators.
- Sailing environment (location, safety provisions etc).

Theory
- Basic theory knowledge is an important requirement as an instructor. A number of methods will be used to assess a candidate's knowledge, including a pre course question paper, multi choice papers and ad hoc informal presentations. Questions will be from an assortment of topics as listed below.

Presentations
- Trainer led discussion on how to deliver a presentation, followed by candidate presentation, aiding development of presentation skills and the ability to deliver appropriate knowledge to course students on the following topics:
  Tides, Sailing Theory, Wind and Weather, Safety, Equipment, Rigging and tuning.

Coaching
- RYA National and Youth Windsurfing Scheme.
- Coaching Adults and Juniors, appropriate equipment, course structure, learning styles.
- Coaching afloat, on-water safety, session planning, skill breakdown, goals, exercises, fault analysis, briefing and debriefing and group control.
- Organisation – On a board and from a coaching boat.
- Windsurfing Specific Rescues (G16 RYA Safety Boat Handbook).
- Instructor Equipment (Safety knives, Buoyancy Aids etc).
- Use of Start Windsurfing method and basic Fastfwd terminology.

Demonstration
- On water demonstrations of On-water 1 and 2.
- On land demonstrations, using a basic simulator, of On-water 1 and 2.

Prior to the course, candidates should ensure they fulfill the following criteria outlined below and within the Start Windsurfing Course information specified on page 24.

Sailing Ability (Pre course requirement)
- RYA Intermediate Non Planing personal certificate.
- Self Assessment Criteria, (prior to the course you must be confident in performing the sailing skills below on appropriate Start Windsurfing Training equipment):
  Stopping and starting under control, close quarters sailing with other board users, NPCG (Non Planing Carve Gybe), flare gybe and faster tacks, sailing on the leeside of the sail, sailing with, and correct use of, a daggerboard, unassisted rigging of a fully battened sail and rescuing a fellow sailor.

Background Knowledge of the Sport
- Windsurfing theory knowledge to an RYA Intermediate level.
- Technical knowledge (we recommend familiarity of up to date windsurfing knowledge through magazines etc).

Intermediate Instructor Training

General Description
The Intermediate course is assessed in two competencies – non planing and planing – and is the first instructor course to incorporate the Fastfwd coaching tool. Candidates will also cover the teaching of all clinics incorporated within the Intermediate syllabus.

Course Information and Content
The course will be run over four days by an RYA Intermediate trainer.

During the Intermediate Windsurfing course a number of different modules will be covered, ensuring sufficient knowledge is gained to teach under the supervision of a Senior Instructor.

Background Knowledge
- RYA schemes, initiatives, Fastfwd coaching model.
- Safeguarding, child protection, health & safety and cold water shock.

Course Management
- Course structure, content and preparation.
- Equipment and simulators, Sailing environment (location, safety provisions etc).

Theory
- Basic theory knowledge is an important requirement as an instructor. A number of methods will be used to assess a candidate's knowledge.

Presentations
- Trainer and candidate lead discussions and presentations, development of presentation skills and the ability to deliver appropriate knowledge to course students on topics such as:
  - Tides, Sailing Theory, Wind and Weather, Safety, Equipment, Rigging and tuning.

Coaching
- Coaching Adults and Juniors, appropriate equipment and use of the syllabus.
- Course structure, learning styles, briefing and debriefing, effective use of racing and freestyle to build skill and confidence.
- Coaching afloat: On-water safety, Session planning, appropriate skill breakdown, goals and exercises, effective use of the coaching model.
- Organisation – On a board and from a coaching boat, Group siting and control.
- Windsurfing Specific Rescues (G16 RYA Safety Boat Handbook).
- Instructor Equipment (Safety knives, Buoyancy Aids etc).
- Coaching ashore: Use of the simulator as a coaching tool, usage and siting, accurate and in-depth understanding of Fastfwd, effective presentation, fault analysis and coaching.

Demonstration
- Accurate on water and land demonstrations and group control (On land and afloat).

Assessment
There is no moderation during the Intermediate Instructor Course. Candidates should be continually assessed by the course.

Course Publications
W4a, W33, W1, G47, G49, G51

Advanced Instructor Training

General Description
The core content of the course enables instructors to teach the main Advanced course in the scheme, including waterstarting and the planing carve gybe. To become an RYA Advanced Plus Instructor, instructors will be assessed on their ability to demonstrate and teach additional Advanced Clinics in carving skills and bump and jump.

Course Information and Content
The course will be run over five days, by an RYA Advanced Trainer.
During the course a number of modules will be covered, ensuring an in depth and confident knowledge is gained to teach under the supervision of a Senior Instructor.

Background Knowledge
- RYA schemes, initiatives, and the RYA Fastfwd coaching model.
- Safeguarding, child protection, health & safety and cold water shock.

Course Management
- Course structure, content and preparation.
- Equipment and simulators, various sailing environments and conditions.

Theory
- A broad and comprehensive knowledge is requirement of an Advanced instructor. A number of methods will be used to assess a candidate's knowledge.

Presentations
- Candidate led discussions and presentations, development of presentation skills and the ability to deliver in depth knowledge to course students on topics such as:
  - Tides, Sailing Theory, Wind and Weather, Safety, Equipment (construction and limitations), Rigging and tuning.

Coaching
- Coaching Adults and Juniors, appropriate equipment and use of the syllabus.
- Course Structure, learning styles and briefing and debriefing.
- Coaching afloat, on-water safety, (including instructor equipment), session planning, skill breakdown, goals, exercises and effective use of the coaching model.
- Organisation – On a board and from a coaching boat, Group siting and control.
- Windsurfing Rescues in high winds and choppy waters (G16 RYA Safety Boat Handbook).
- Coaching ashore: Use of the simulator as a coaching tool, usage and siting, an accurate and in-depth understanding of the Fastfwd Formula, fault analysis and coaching.

Demonstration
- Accurate on water and land demonstrations and group control (on land and afloat).

Assessment
There is no moderation during the Intermediate Instructor Course. Candidates should be continually assessed by the course trainer.

Course Publications
W4a, W33, W1, G47, G49, G51 and G52

Senior Instructor Training

The Principal of an RYA Training Centre carries the formal responsibility for ensuring that all training complies with RYA guidelines, laid down in the current "Guidance Notes for Inspection of RYA Recognised Training Centres". An RYA recognised windsurfing training centre must have a current SI as its Principal or Chief Windsurfing Instructor. The Principal may be a Senior Instructor or may appoint a Senior Instructor to act as Windsurfing Chief Instructor to ensure that windsurfing tuition is organised according to RYA teaching methods and standards.

The Senior Instructor (SI) is an experienced instructor who has been assessed as competent to organise and manage courses within the RYA's schemes. They are qualified to organise and control group tuition, and to supervise and assist instructors. A SI needs to be patient, and resourceful, as well as being a confident, competent manager, capable of organising groups of all ages and abilities, and directing the work of their instructors. They also need the organisational ability to ensure that courses are enjoyable, safe and informative. The SI will be expected to: plan and organise sessions, and brief, run and debrief exercises.

Apart from responsibility to students, the SI has a responsibility to their instructors, to the club or employer and the RYA. A Windsurfing SI should be capable of managing and supervising one or more groups afloat, each group taught by an appropriately qualified instructor. They need understanding of the full requirements of RYA Training Centre recognition and, where necessary, put in place all the necessary systems and documentation. This may well include carrying out or revising a risk assessment, and specifying and recording safety procedures.

Course Organisation
Duration: Four day course which can be run over two weekends. The course may run at two different locations, within the same region, to provide the candidates with the opportunity to work at different centres and under different operating procedures.
Run by: Minimum of two RYA Windsurfing Trainers

When planning the course, the organising trainers should try to ensure there are mixtures of candidates from differing teaching backgrounds. This will encourage candidates to learn from each other's experiences, and help them to discuss and solve problems throughout the course.

Content: SI Training needs to consist of, not only discussions and tasks, with specialist input from the course trainers, but also with the experiences of others in the group. For this reason the organising trainers will look carefully at the profile of each SI candidate.

Practical Sessions
The course is based on continual assessment and will be packed with practical sessions. These sessions are chosen by the trainers but planned, organised and run by the individual candidates, making the course intense, but informative.

Each session will be conducted by a course candidate who will brief the group, run the session and then debrief the group when finished. The rest of the course candidates take differing roles, such as instructor's assistants, group members being taught or the designated SI for that session.

Practical sessions designated by the course trainers should begin with any part of the Start Windsurfing syllabus of the National Scheme and, as confidence in delivery grows, other appropriate areas of the National and Youth Scheme syllabus should be used.

These sessions provide a great opportunity for candidates to refresh and improve their skills, giving the course candidates a range of short sessions delivered in a variety of ways.

Built into each practical session should be the opportunity to develop the student's ability to brief and debrief, whether to a group of students or as an SI to their instructors. At the beginning of the four days, the course trainers should offer a model for the candidates to build on. For further information on briefing and debriefing, and how to gain the most from it, see pages 54-57.

On the completion of each session, the course trainer should debrief the whole group on the way the session was managed, enabling each candidate to learn from each session run.

Theoretical Sessions

During the course, candidates should build on their ability to manage and supervise one or more groups afloat. They should also understand the full requirements of RYA training centre recognition and the necessary systems and documentation, such as operating procedures. Prior to the course candidates must complete the Senior Instructor Workbook, which will support discussions during the course and encourage the candidates to start thinking along the lines of an SI.

The workbook contains a number of different exercises on topics such as session planning, risk assessment, operational procedures and briefing and debriefing. Some of these topics can also be given to the candidates to deliver during the course as presentations or chaired workshop discussions. This workbook may initially appear to be rather daunting but, having prepared for the course by completing this document, most candidates appreciate its value.

By bringing a variety of candidates together on a course there will be a real mixture of experiences. Running a session on catastrophes enables students to outline the worst things which have happened to them while teaching. The group can consider each example discussing ways in which the problem could be solved or avoided.

A useful summary of this session is to discuss any recurring themes, such as equipment failure, weather forecasting and undisclosed health problems and know to limit or control their effect on our sessions.

Assessment

The assessment on a Senior Instructor course is continual. Here are just a few areas a course trainer will be looking at:

- Ability to plan, organise and run practical sessions with a clear session brief, clear aims, objectives, safety brief including signals and an identified sailing area.
- Whole group involvement:
  - On-water coaching.
  - Group control.
  - Objectives achieved.
  - Clear and informative feedback in the debrief.
- Active input during shorebased sessions.
- Ability to observe sessions and then debrief instructors.
- Ability to be a team player and role model.

In addition to the above requirements, the course trainer will apply consideration based on their experience of the scheme and whether each candidate meets the requirements of a Senior Instructor. Should they be unable to confirm that a candidate has successfully completed the course, the trainer will outline the reasons for the decision and compile an action plan.

Racing Instructor Course

Duration: 2 days
Run by RYA Racing Instructor Tutor

This course is pitched at existing RYA windsurfing instructors who have little to no competition experience in either windsurfing or dinghy sailing. The content of the RYA Racing Instructor Manual forms the basis for this instructor course.

The course hopes to encourage more instructors to get involved in setting up and running club level competition as a way of engaging windsurfers of all ages on a regular basis. By offering grassroots competition training, club level sailors are put at ease regarding what to expect and how to get around a course easily.

The Racing Instructor course also provides further information on what the Team15 programme is trying to achieve at both club level and at the inter-club challenges. It explains in detail the Team15 philosophy and the teaching method behind the programme.

It is recommended that, prior to attending the Racing Instructor course, candidates have taught at least 2-3 Start Windsurfing courses – adults or juniors – since group control is essential.

The Racing Instructor, although responsible for teaching individuals, small groups and Team15 club sessions, has not been assessed as competent in running a windsurfing centre and should always work under the supervision of an RYA Senior Instructor. Once qualified, a Racing Instructor is qualified to teach the Start Racing syllabus to all age groups.

Course Content

To assist the Racing Instructor in delivering suitable sessions relevant to the Start Racing syllabus, the Racing Instructor Manual has been written to provide useful background information to each topic, supported by session plans with approximate delivery times. These include topics such as:

- Background to UK racing set up and opportunities for adults and children.
- The RYA competition pathway.
- RYA Schemes: How to use these within Team15 clubs and at a wider club level.
- Types of competition and courses.
- Basic racing rules and the start procedure.
- Understanding wind shadows.
- Mark rounding, effective tacking and gybing.
- Weather forecasting, tides, equipment choice and tuning techniques.
- Equipment preparation.
- Health and nutrition.

Course Publications

W3, W1

RYA Windsurfing Instructor Qualification Log

RYA Training Qualifications

RYA Assistant Instructor

RYA Assistant Instructor			
Personal Sailing Assessment	Level: (Intermediate Non Planing or above)		Tidal/Non Tidal
	Centre:		
Valid First Aid	Type:		Expiry Date:
RYA Powerboat Level 2 Certificate	Tidal/Non Tidal:		
	Centre:		

Dates:	Centre:
Principal/CI:	Signed:

Action Plan / Comments:

Tidal/Non Tidal

RYA Start Instructor

RYA Start Instructor			
Personal Sailing Assessment	Level: (Intermediate Non Planing or above)		Tidal/Non Tidal
	Centre:		
Valid First Aid	Type:		Expiry Date:
RYA Powerboat Level 2 Certificate	Tidal/Non Tidal:		
	Centre:		

Dates:	Centre:
Trainer:	Signed:
Moderator:	Signed:
Principal:	Signed:

Action Plan / Comments:

Tidal/Non Tidal

RYA Intermediate Instructor

RYA Intermediate Instructor		
Personal Sailing Assessment	Intermediate Instructor Non Planing/Planing (Delete as appropriate) (Intermediate Planing or above) Centre:	Tidal/Non Tidal
Valid First Aid	Type:	Expiry Date:
RYA Powerboat Level 2 Certificate	Tidal/Non Tidal: Centre:	

Dates:	Centre:
Trainer:	Signed:
Principal:	Signed:
Action Plan/Comments:	
Tidal/Non Tidal	

Completion of Intermediate Planing Instructor

Please use the following box in the event of upgrading your Intermediate Non-Planing Instructor qualification to Intermediate Planing at a later stage, or on completion of an action plan.

Dates:	Centre:
Trainer:	Signed:
Principal:	Signed:
Action Plan/Comments:	
Tidal/Non Tidal	

RYA Advanced Instructor

RYA Advanced Instructor			
Personal Sailing Assessment	Advanced Instructor/Advanced Plus (Delete as appropriate)		
	(Advanced or above)		Tidal/Non Tidal
	Centre:		
Valid First Aid	Type:		Expiry Date:
RYA Powerboat Level 2 Certificate	Tidal/Non Tidal:		
	Centre:		

Dates:	Centre:
Trainer:	Signed:
Principal:	Signed:
Action Plan/Comments:	
Tidal/Non Tidal	

Completion of Advanced Plus Instructor
Please use the following box in the event of upgrading your Advanced Instructor qualification to Advanced Plus at a later stage, or on completion of an action plan.

Dates:	Centre:
Trainer:	Signed:
Principal:	Signed:
Action Plan/Comments:	
Tidal/Non Tidal	

RYA Senior Instructor

RYA Senior Instructor			
Personal Sailing Assessment			Tidal/Non Tidal
	Centre:		
Valid First Aid	Type:		Expiry Date:
RYA Safety Boat Certificate	Tidal/Non Tidal:		
	Centre:		

RYA Centre Principal Nomination

Name: Signed:

Principal's Comments:

Course Results

Dates:	Centre:
Trainer (1):	Signed:
Trainer (2):	Signed:
Principal:	

Tidal/Non Tidal

Racing Qualifications

RYA Racing Instructor

Personal Sailing Assessment	Level: (Intermediate Non Planing or above)		Tidal/Non Tidal
	Centre:		
Valid First Aid	Type:	Expiry Date:	
RYA Powerboat Level 2 Certificate	Tidal/Non Tidal:		
	Centre:		

Dates:	Centre:
Trainer/Tutor:	Signed:
Principal:	Signed:
Comments:	

RYA Level 2 Race Coach

Personal Sailing Assessment	Level: (Intermediate Non Planing or above)		Tidal/Non Tidal
	Centre:		
Valid First Aid	Type:		Expiry Date:
RYA Powerboat Level 2 Certificate	Tidal/Non Tidal:		
	Centre:		

Dates:	Centre:
Trainer/Tutor:	Signed:
Action Plan/Comments:	
Tidal/Non Tidal	

RYA Level 3 Race Coach

Personal Sailing Assessment	Level: (Intermediate Non Planing or above)		Tidal/Non Tidal
	Centre:		
Valid First Aid	Type:		Expiry Date:
RYA Powerboat Level 2 Certificate	Tidal/Non Tidal:		
	Centre:		

Dates:	Centre:
Trainer/Tutor:	Signed:
Principal:	Signed:
Action Plan/Comments:	
Tidal/Non Tidal	

Teaching Experience and Log

The following pages are to record your personal teaching experiences. Entries should be accompanied by the Principal's signature and RYA Training Centre name. This evidence of teaching experience is essential to allow you to be considered for attendance on more advanced courses and revalidations.

Date & Level of Group	Session (Inc. Hours Logged & Equipment used)	Weather Conditions	Training Centre & Principal's Signature

Resources and References

As mentioned throughout this book, there are a number of additional RYA publications that may complement, enhance and act as further reading through your career as an instructor.

Here are just a few. All books listed can be purchased direct from the RYA webshop.

RYA Code	Title
G47	RYA National Windsurfing Scheme Syllabus & Logbook
G49	RYA Start Windsurfing
G51	RYA Intermediate Windsurfing
G52	RYA Advanced Windsurfing
W1	RYA Youth Windsurfing Scheme Syllabus & Logbook
G16	RYA Safety Boat Handbook
ZF03	St John Ambulance First Aid Manual
G1	RYA Weather Handbook (Northern Hemisphere Edition)

Active Learning	Students involving themselves fully with enthusiasm
Auditory Learning	Students who relate well to spoken word
Battened Rig	A sail with stiff flexible rods giving strength and shape
Blasting	Moving quickly across water
Boom	The 'handlebars' of a windsurfer
Broad Reach	Direction approximately 135° away from the direction of the wind
Bump and Jump	Action for getting airborne
Butterfly method	A form of self-rescue
Carve Gybe	Gybing in breezy/windy conditions
Chop Hop	An action to become airborne
Downhaul	Rope used to attach the tack of a sail to the mastfoot, enabling rig turning
Drop and Dig/Push	Dynamic body position (stance)
FastFwd Formula	National windsurfing coaching model
Flagging	A form of self-rescue used to go downwind
Goal point	A point chosen to aim for when sailing
Hamburger	Feedback model
Killcord	Safety lanyard that cuts out the engine in an emergency
Kinaesthetic Learning	Students who learn well through touch and movement
Lift and Lock	Body position (stance)
Mast foot	Flexible joint between mast and board
Nose over Toes	A body action when beachstarting
OnBoard	Nationwide programme for young people to go sailing
Outhaul	Rope attaching the clew of the sail to end of boom
Planing	Where board reaches sufficient speed to travel on surface of water
PowerPoint	Computer-based visual presentation system
Pragmatists	Students who think that if it works, it's good
Reflection	Technique for answering students' questions
Reflective Learners	Students who ponder experiences and observe from different perspectives
Rig	Sail, mast and boom (also verb for assembling them)
Rig Elevation	Sliding the mast to windward as rig elevated
Rig Rotator	A specific action during gybe
Rig Twisting	Rig action during a beachstart
Rigging Sticks	Wind awareness and basic board control teaching aids
Sailability	RYA sailing scheme for people with disabilities
Shifting and Switching	Movement of feet during tacking and gybing
Slide and Glide	Rig action during a beach or waterstart
Stance	Body position while sailing
Straight 7	A specific body position (stance)
Team15	Network of clubs for windsurfers aged 15 or under
Traffic Light	Feedback model
Trim	Ensuring the board is kept flat
Tuning	Correct setup of board and rig for conditions
Uphaul	Combined rope and elastic attached to the boom enabling rig to be pulled out of the water
Visual Preference	Students relate well to written information, pictures etc.
Volvo Champion clubs	Scheme recognising high junior training standards